I can draw

A STEP BY STEP GUIDE FOR TEACHERS

Written and Illustrated
by
Jan Evans

First Published
May 2006 in Great Britain by

PRINT

Educational Printing Services Limited

Albion Mill, Water Street, Great Harwood, Blackburn, BB6 7QR
Telephone: (01245) 882080   Fax: (01254)882010
E-mail: enquiries@eprint.co.uk   Website: www.eprint.co.uk

ISBN I 904904 79 3

Contents

Introduction

Being firmly of the belief that everyone can be taught to draw . . .
the aim of this book is to provide teachers with easy to follow lesson plans for activities that teach children how to draw in a developmental way. Whilst skills are often reinforced, they are also extended progressively through the book. They can be applied to all ages.

The key element is to teach mark making skills that are implemented through a wide range of activities and using different tools and media.
The activities also include the development of observational skills and nurturing a greater understanding of line, texture and form.

There are step by step illustrations for each activity.
Snapshots are provided to give a brief outline of each lesson giving a quick overview without having to read the whole lesson plan.
With some activities, the work of well known artists can be used as added stimulus and for reference, to highlight styles and techniques.

The activities cover the requirements of the programmes of study for Art and Design in the National Curriculum both by introducing children to a range of materials and tools, but also by developing appropriate skills, knowledge and understanding. As children often record by drawing the step by step guides are useful for other curriculum areas.

The first five lessons teach basic drawing skills and develop understanding about texture, shape and form. I strongly recommend all of these are taught as they teach very fundamental skills.
The rest of the book provides a range of activities to reinforce these skills and introduce a range of techniques. These can be dipped into rather than working through lesson by lesson.

Most materials used should be readily available in any well resourced art stock cupboard. Others are easily available.

Photocopiable templates are provided at the end of the book and some larger colour photos to use as starting points.

Contents

Making a Mark

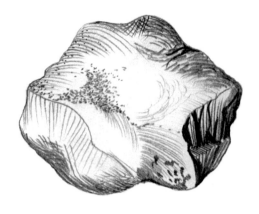

Activity 1

Activity 2

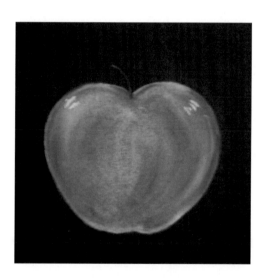

Activity 3

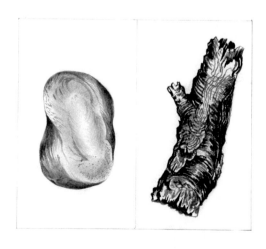

Activity 4

Activity 5

Making a Mark

Introduction

Art work is made up of marks. Whatever tools are used, the information is communicated through a variety of different marks.
The first five lessons teach some very fundamental drawing skills finding out how to apply marks to visually describe an object.
In each lesson the skills used for both the warm up and main activity are modelled to the children.

They also encourage children to look closely at objects so that they can learn:

- How to identify and draw the main shapes.

- How to use marks to visually describe the texture.

- How to create form so that an object looks 3D.

It is highly recommended that the five lessons are taught in succession before moving on to the other activities.
Although they may not seem very creative, they teach key foundational skills that are extended and developed throughout the rest of the book.

Snapshot   Making a Mark 1

To learn how to make different marks.
To look closely at the shape and texture of an object and use marks to represent the texture.

Observational drawing   <u>Medium:</u>   Pencil

Warm up Activity

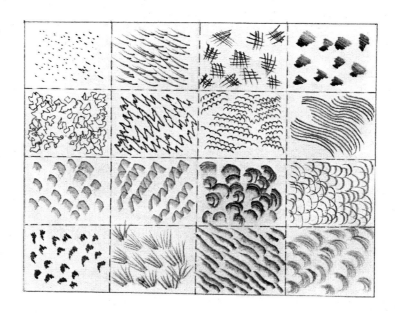

Main Activity

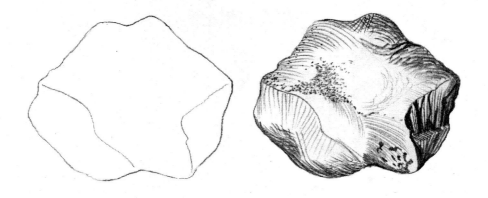

Making a Mark

Objectives   To learn how to make different marks.
To look closely at the shape and texture of an object and use different marks to represent texture.

Resources   Paper, HB pencils
Natural objects: stones, shells, wood etc.
Magnifying glasses

Warm up Activity

1. Fold a piece of paper four times to create sixteen sections (Differentiate by reducing or increasing e.g. eight or thirty-two.

2. Each section is going to have a different kind of mark.
None can be the same!
They could be dots, dashes, lines, squirls etc.
Demonstrate how to use the point or side of the lead and how to vary pressure from light to firm (see example).

Main Activity

1. Choose an object with a definite texture.
Ask the children to describe what they can see in terms of shape and texture.
Draw the shape.

2. Show how to make it look rough, bumpy etc. by using different marks, pressing lightly/firmly (refer to examples on warm up sheet).
Use magnifying glass to look more closely.

    Children choose from a range of natural objects and with reference to their 'warm up' sheet make marks that best represent the texture (see example).

Evaluation   Either as whole class or in groups children can try and identify which objects others have drawn by 'matching the marks/shapes of each others drawings to the objects.

Snapshot   Making a Mark 2

To understand that the way lines and marks are used creates the shape and form of the object.

Drawing of fruit using line drawing/shading   <u>Medium:</u> Pencil

Warm up Activity

Main Activity

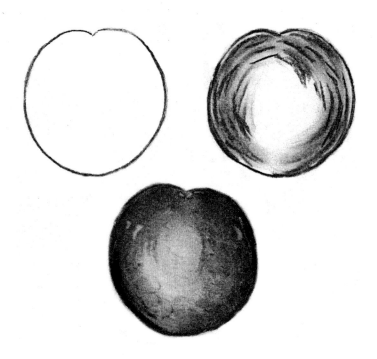

Making a Mark

Objective   To understand that the way lines and marks are used helps to create shape and form.

Resources   Paper
Pencils
Charcoal and cotton buds (optional but less messy)
Fruit: apples, oranges, pears, grapes

Warm up Activity

This activity is carried out step by step with children copying each step.

Fold a piece of paper into four and draw four apples.

Apple 1. Draw straight vertical lines.

Apple 2. Draw straight horizontal lines.

Apple 3. Draw curved vertical lines following shape.

Apple 4. Draw curved horizontal lines following shape.

See if children can identify/describe the difference.
The way we apply lines/marks makes the apple look round/3D.

Main Activity

1.   Select a piece of fruit. Draw outline shape with charcoal.

2.   Begin to create form with curved marks that follow the shape. Use your finger or a cotton bud to smudge, using curved movements to make the fruit look round/3D.

3.   Darken the marks around the edge and leave the centre lighter. This also helps create the form. Adding white highlights enhances the drawing makes the skins shiny!
Children select several fruits for their own drawing, main focus to make the shape look round, not flat! (3D not 2D)

Evaluation   Can you tell which fruit it is? Does it look round or flat?
How did you make it look like that?

To use curved marks to make an object look round.
To use tones of colour to help create form.

Drawing fruit   Medium: Chalks

Warm up Activity

Main Activity

Making a Mark

Objectives   To used curved marks to make an object look round.
To use tones of colour to help create form.

Resources   Rough white paper, black paper (A4)
Charcoal, chalks, cotton buds, rubbers
Selection of fruit: apples, oranges, pears

Warm up Activity

This activity reinforces the main activity from lesson 2.

1.   On a rough piece of paper draw a circle with charcoal.
Point out that it looks a round flat shape.

2.   Starting at the edge of the circle curve marks around the shape.
Smudge with finger/cotton bud, leaving the centre lighter. Add
more charcoal to darken the edges.

Main Activity

Select a fruit. A Granny Smith's apple is used here.

1.   On the black paper draw a light outline of an apple, filling most of
the page.

2.   Using the side of a bright green chalk, curve marks around the
edges of the apple on both sides. Use a finger or cotton bud to
blend towards the centre reinforcing curved movements.

3.   Point out where the light is on the apple and where the colour
looks darker.

Use a lighter green/yellow to add some colour to the centre and
blend in. Add small amounts of dark green around the edges and
blend. The use of light and dark colours adds to the 3D effect.

4.   Identify where the light shines on the skin. Add a small curve of
white. This makes the skin look shiny. Use a rubber to clean
smudges and redefine lines.

Evaluation   Does the fruit look round? How did we make it look 3D?

To learn that there are different grades of pencils.
To use marks to create rough or smooth textures.

Observational drawing   Medium: Pencil

Warm up Activity

Main Activity

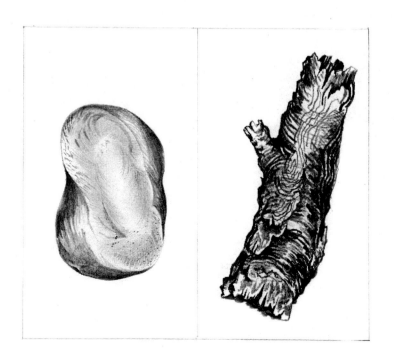

Making a Mark

Objectives To learn that there are different grades of pencils.
To use marks to create rough or smooth textures.

Resources Range of lead pencils: 2H, HB, 3B, 6B.
Rough paper, Cartridge paper
Range of rough/smooth objects
E.g. smooth pebble/shell/wood
rough stone/shell/bark/pine cone

Warm up Activity

Explain that there are different grades of pencils.
Pencils with an H have a hard lead, the higher the number the harder the lead and a more silvery colour.
Pencils with a B have a softer and more smudgy lead, the higher the number the softer and darker the lead.
On the rough paper ask children to try out different pencils to see the variation, and to try and make marks that look either rough or smooth.

Main Activity

1. Fold a piece of cartridge paper in half. Choose one rough and one smooth object. Draw the shapes lightly for each one with are most appropriate for each object.
    Generally, softer leads for rougher textures, harder for smoother ones.

2. Demonstrate how to use marks to create the texture for the rough shape, and smoother shading for the smooth one.
    Children then select two objects of their own and decide for themselves which pencils are most appropriate.

Evaluation Do the objects look rough or smooth? Were the right pencils/marks used?

Snapshot   Making a Mark 5

Learn how to draw 3D shapes.
To learn how to apply tones of colour to add to the form.

Drawing regular 3D shapes   <u>Medium:</u>   Charcoal, Chalks

Warm up Activity

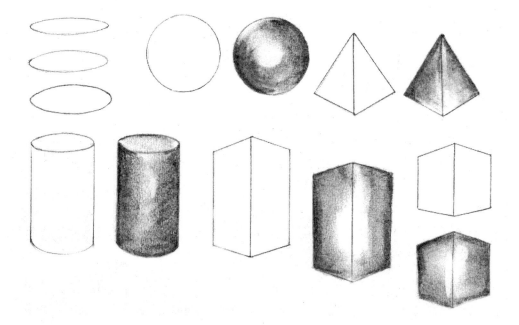

Main Activity

Making a Mark

Objective   *To learn how to draw 3D shapes.*
To learn how to apply tones of colour to add to the form.

Resources   A4 paper: rough/black sugar paper
Charcoal
Chalks
3D shapes: geometric maths shapes/boxes/tins/candles
For the purpose of this activity it is better if the shapes are plain so
children aren't distracted by the graphics.

Warm up Activity

On rough paper practice drawing ellipses (see example).
Demonstrate how to draw a cylinder, make sure the base is curved
too.
Demonstrate how to draw cube/cuboid/pyramid/sphere.

Ask does the sphere look round? How could we make it appear
round?

Using skills from previous sessions use charcoal to shade.
Shade other shapes making them darker on the furthest edges and
lighter on the nearer ones.

Main Activity

Select one of the 3D shapes. On black paper draw the shape lightly
as demonstrated in the warm up activity.

Select light and dark of the same colour (e.g. blue).
Starting at the furthest edges use the flat side of the darker blue to
shade. If a cylinder is used, make sure the marks are curved.

Use the lighter colour as you move towards the nearest edge. Blend
the colours.

Finally add white to highlight.

Evaluation   Can you tell which shape it is? Does it look 3D? How did you
make it look 3D?

Still Life

Activity 1

Activity 2

Activity 3

Activity 4

Activity 5

Activity 6

Still Life
Drawing from Observation
Introduction

The following six lessons are covering the same basic objectives encouraging children to look closely at objects and to apply the skills taught in the 'Mark Making' lessons. Each lesson can be taught in isolation or selected to fit in with particular topics. They are designed to reinforce basic skills and are successful in developing understanding of shape, form and composition.

- Demonstration

    Each activity requires a demonstration to take the children through the steps.

    No part of the drawing needs to be completed during whole class teaching.

    Once the outline has been drawn it is sufficient to demonstrate techniques and how to create the desired effect, in part.

- Reinforce

    - Drawing lightly so that mistakes can be rubbed out easily.
    - Filling the whole page, children nearly always want to do a small drawing in the centre!
    - Using marks to create form. Curved marks following a shape really do make an object look round.
    - How to apply colour using light and darker shades of the same colour to show light and dark on the object.
    - Highlights of white make object looks shiny.

The work of Cézanne provides some excellent examples of still life paintings. They are helpful in encouraging children to think about composition and colour.

Snapshot   Still Life 1

To learn to look at shape and form by close observation of an object.
To be able to create a soft furry texture.

Drawing of a soft toy   <u>Medium:</u> Pencil

Still Life
Drawing from Observation

Objectives   *To learn to look at shape and form by close observation of an object.*
To be able to create a soft furry texture.

Resources   Range of pencils H - 4B, rubbers
Cartridge paper (A4/A3)
Variety of soft toys
Using chalks or oil pastels as an alternative provides a good extension activity

Activity   To draw a toy that looks soft and furry.

Demonstrate how to create the shape and form of the selected toy by following the step by step guide.
In this example the bear is in a seated position.

1. Using H/HB pencil lightly draw in main shapes of head, body and arms.
Reinforce making light marks, so mistakes can easily be erased, but also in this case the edges need to be soft and furry.

2. Demonstrate how to draw feet. They look larger as they are further forward and most of the leg cannot be seen.

3. Add ears, eyes, nose. Eyes and nose can be made to look shiny by leaving a small area of white.
Choose a softer leaded pencil to start making marks for the fur. Follow the shapes of the body parts to create form. Allow marks to go over original shapes to give the impression of fur.

4. Begin to show perspective and a more 3D form by shading in darker areas.
Use a rubber to create some highlights.

Evaluation   Does the toy look soft and furry? Does it have a 3D shape?

To accurately draw objects from observation. To be able to use marks to create appearance of different surfaces.

Drawing wooden/metal objects   <u>Medium:</u> Pencil

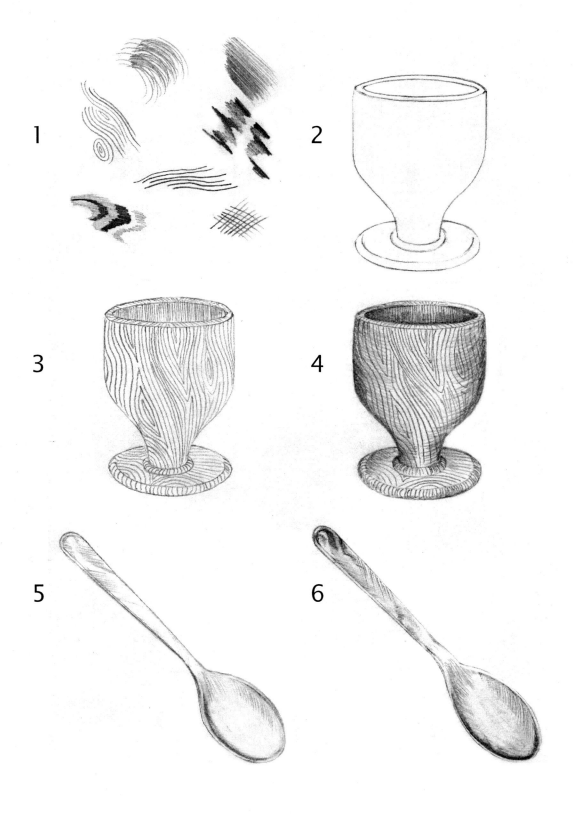

1

2

3

4

5

6

Still Life

Drawing from Observation

Objectives   *To accurately draw objects from observation.*
To be able to use marks to create appearance of different surfaces.

Resources   Range of pencils 2H – 2B, rubbers
Cartridge paper (A4)
Wooden objects: wooden spoon/bowl/box etc.
Metal objects: scissors/cutlery/tin opener etc.

Activity   To draw a wooden object and a metal object.

Drawings could be done on the same piece of paper or on two separate pieces.
Remind children of different effects of graded pencils and use of marks to create texture.

1. Discuss surfaces/texture of different objects and think how they could be represented by marks. (see example 1)
   Demonstrate a few ideas.

2. Select a wooden object. With H/HB pencil lightly draw the shape.

3. Use HB/B to make lines and marks to create a wood grain effect.

4. Remember where a shape is rounded to curve marks and add shading to create form.

5. Select a metal object. Using H pencil lightly draw the shape.
   The effect of metal is created by a contrast between areas of light and dark because of the reflections on the surface.

6. Use different pencils to show the contrast. Marks and shading need to be smooth and curved where a rounded effect is required.

Evaluation   Can we tell which are the metal/wooden objects?
Can we see the texture of the wood? Do the metal objects look smooth and shiny?

Snapshot   Still Life 3

To draw a collection of objects from observation.
To think about composition and use of space.

Drawing vegetables

Medium: Oil pastel

1

2

3

4

Still Life
Drawing from Observation

Objectives   *To draw a collection of objects from observation.*
To think about composition and use of space.

Resources   Black sugar paper (A3)
Light coloured pencils: white/yellow
Oil pastels
Selection of vegetables: peppers (good because of vibrant colours and shapes) mushrooms/onions etc.

Activity   To draw a composition of vegetables.

Arrange vegetables to create composition.

1.   Using white or yellow pencil lightly draw the outline shapes. Show children how to draw shapes that are in front of each other. Point out that nearer objects 'hide' parts of the ones behind.

2.   Start with the vegetables at the back of the picture and use same principles for applying colour as in 'Making a Mark Lesson 3'. That is darker and lighter shades of the same colour to create the form, and curved marks to show rounded shapes. The darker colour is used where there is shadow, and the lighter where the light is on the object. Gradually work towards the foreground.

3.   If colours in the foreground are brighter and more intense it helps to create perspective. The darker duller shapes recede, brighter lighter shapes come forward.
Add small white highlights to make the skin look shiny.

Evaluation   Ask children to make positive and constructive comments about each others work. Do the vegetables look real/round?
Do they look like they are in front/behind each other?

Snapshot   Still Life 4

To look carefully at the main shapes of objects.
To copy specific details of an object.

Drawing shoes   <u>Medium:</u> Pencil

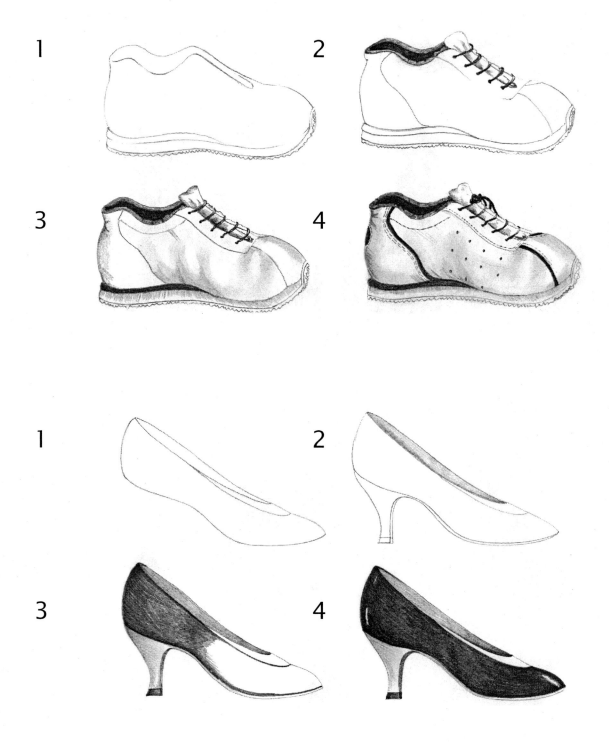

24

Still Life
Drawing from Observation

Objectives To look carefully at the main shapes of objects.
To copy specific details of an object.

Resources Cartridge paper (A3)
HB pencils, rubbers
Colouring pencils
Variety of shoes

Activity To make a detailed drawing of a shoe.

Example: Trainer
1. Lightly draw outline of the basic shape so that it fills most of the paper.

2. Add perspective by drawing inside, tongue/laces.

3. Identify areas of shadow and light.

4. Begin to add details such as colour/stripes/logo.
Darken areas of colour to help create 3D form.

Example: Heeled Shoe
1. Lightly draw outline of the basic shape so that it fills most of the paper.

2. Draw in the heel and the inside of the shoe.

3. Use curved marks/shading to create rounded shape of the shoe.

4. Leaving small areas of white make the shoe look shiny.
Add any details, e.g. stitching, buckles etc.

Evaluation Encourage children to discuss why they think their drawings have been successful and to identify the use of particular skills.

To be able to draw objects in front of one another. To use marks and colour to create form.

Medium: Chalks

Teapot, cups and saucers

1

2

3

4

26

Still Life

Drawing from Observation

Objectives   *To draw a collection of objects from observation.*
To use marks and colour to create form.

Resources   Black sugar paper (A3), rubbers
Coloured chalks (thin small sticks are preferable)
Crockery/teapot/cups/saucers (biscuits)

Activity   To draw composition of teapot/cups.

1. Use white chalk to lightly draw outline of basic shape of teapot. (Chalk can be rubbed out!)
Add handle and spout. Objects need to be large enough to fill the page. This always needs reinforcing.

2. Remind children about ellipses and draw shapes for saucers (and biscuits if applicable) and cups, remembering shapes in the foreground may obscure shapes in the background.

3. It is important with chalk to work from the top of the page down to avoid smudging.
Begin to apply colour as in 'Mark Making' Lesson 3 starting with objects in the background.
Use darker and lighter shades of the same colour to create the form and curved marks to show rounded shapes. The darker colour is used where there is shadow and the lighter where the light is on the object.
Gradually work towards the foreground.

4. White chalk can be added for extra contrast and highlights.
Finally, details are added such as pattern on cups, biscuits.
Rubbers can be used to clean up any smudges.

Evaluation   Does the composition fill the page? Does the teapot look round.
Are the cups the right size next to the teapot?

Snapshot   Still Life 6   To be able to observe details. To be able to match colours and design.

Medium: Chalks

Sweet wrappers

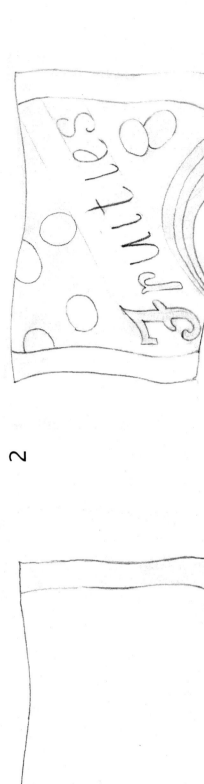

1

2

3

4

Still Life
Drawing from Observation

Objectives   To be able to observe details.
                 To be able to match colours and design.

Resources   Cartridge paper A4
                 HB pencils
                 Rubbers
                 Wide range of colouring pencils
                 Selection of packets/cartons (Sweets have proved to be the most successful)

Activity   To copy packaging designs.

                 Select a packet.

1.   <u>Lightly</u> draw the outline of the shape.
       This may require reminding children how to draw a cylinder or cuboid.
       Talk to children about the size of the writing/logo/pictures of the sweets etc.

2.   Mark out where the writing is going to go and other key shapes.
       Refer back to the packet to compare proportions of different parts of the design.
       Demonstrate how to do lettering (see example).

3.   Draw in other key features of the packaging.
       Find colours that are the best match.

4.   Demonstrate how to colour different areas of the packaging.
       Remind children about leaving small white areas as highlights e.g. on lettering.

Evaluation   Compare drawings to original packets.
                 Encourage children to find areas that have worked well, or ways in which improvements could be made.

People

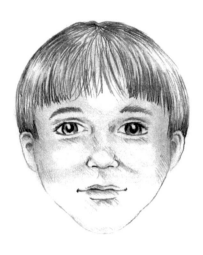

Activity 1

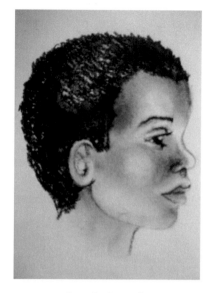

Activity 2

Activity 3

Activity 4

Activity 5

People

Introduction

The following five lessons look at how to draw people in proportion.
The first three focus on the face, looking firstly at how to draw a portrait, then a profile and finally looking at expressions. These lessons have been used very successfully with young children right through to adults.

The last two lessons focus on drawing the whole body. They are generally more appropriate from Year 2. It is difficult for younger children to grasp the proportions and measurements of the whole body.
The drawings are based on creating a frame as an aid to drawing the body proportions correctly. This frame is described as a skeletal structure as the key shapes relate to the rib area, spine, pelvis etc.

- A very successful extension activity to drawing the whole body is to use the work of well known artists to copy from:

- Picasso   Child with a dove
- Toulouse – Lautrec   Woman seated in the garden
- Mary Cassat   Two children playing on the beach
- Renoir   La Danse à Bougival
- Degas   Dancer at the bar
- Cézanne   Louis Auguste Cézanne's father
- Diego Rivera   Retrato de Ignacio Sanchez
- Amadeo Modigliani   Boy in blue

To draw a face (portrait) with correct proportions.

Portrait drawing   <u>Medium:</u> Pencil

1

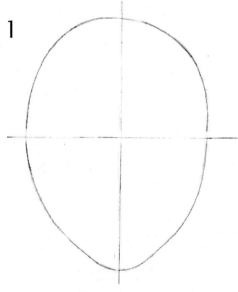

Draw an egg shape that is rounder at the top and narrower at the bottom. <u>Lightly</u> draw a line down the centre and a line across the middle dividing the face into quarters.

2

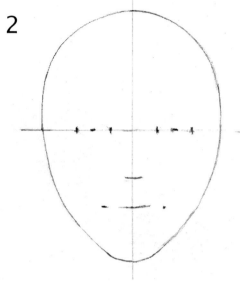

Mark the eyes half way down the face on the horizontal line. (with an 'eye space' between) Mark the centre of the nose on the vertical line. The corners of the mouth should line up with the centre of the eyes. Leave enough space for the chin.

3

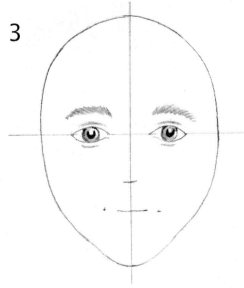

Draw the eyes. They are oval (lemon) shape. Draw the iris and the pupils. Leave a white spot to make eyes look shiny. Eyelids and eyebrows can be added.

4

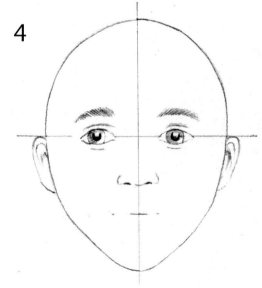

The nose is as wide as the space between the eyes. Draw two bracket shapes for the side of the nose and two small curves for the nostrils.
The top of the ears are level with the eyes and the bottom level with the end of the nose.

People

Objectives   To be able to draw a portrait.
To learn the correct proportions for drawing a face.

Resources   Cartridge paper
HB pencils, rubbers

5   Draw the centre line of the mouth.
The bottom lip is curved and the top
one straighter. Draw the cheek lines
from the nose to the mouth.
Rub out the guidelines.

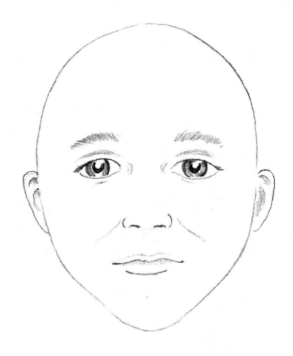

6   Give the face shape by shading the sides
of the forehead, the edges of the cheeks
and the sides of the nose. Leave a light
area as highlight in the centre of the
forehead, cheeks, chin and end of the
nose. Add hair using curved marks to
accentuate the round shape of the head.

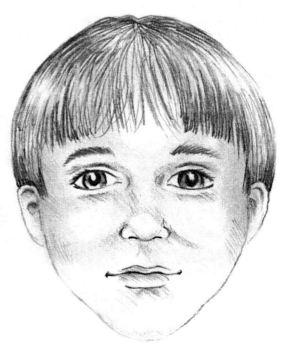

Evaluation   Is the face in proportion?
Does it look 3D?

35

Snapshot   People 2

To draw a face (profile) with correct proportions.

Drawing a profile   <u>Medium:</u> Charcoal

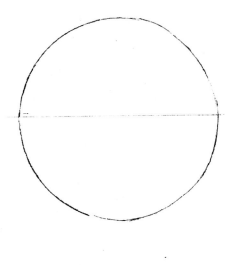

1 Draw a circle with a guideline halfway down.

2 Draw the lines of the neck and add in the chin which is level with the forehead.

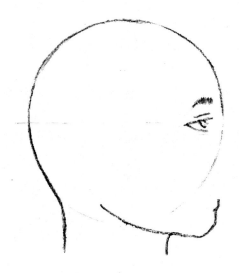

3 Draw in the eye.
   Note the shape of the eye from the side.
   Mark in the eyebrow and eyelid.

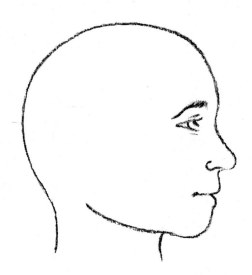

4 Draw the nose and the mouth. The eye is level with the bridge of the nose.

People

Objectives *To be able to draw a profile.*
To learn the correct proportions for drawing a face.

Resources Cartridge paper or light coloured paper.
Charcoal, rubbers

5   Add details to the eye, (leaving a white
spot makes it look shiny) and complete
the mouth. Shade the face as shown to
create a round shape.

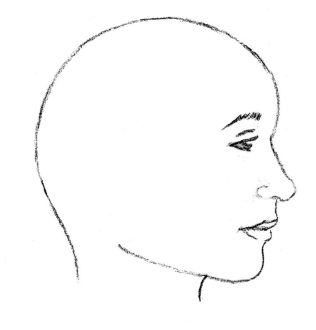

6   Draw a 'C' shape for the ear towards the
centre of the circle. The top of the ear is
level with the eye, and the bottom with
the mouth. Add the hair, using curved
marks to show the rounded shape of the
head.

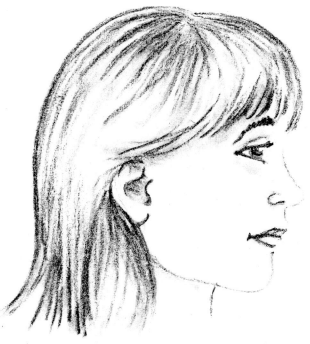

Evaluation Is the eye the right shape? Does the head look 3D?

Snapshot   People 3

To be able to daw a face in proportion.
To draw faces showing different expressions.

Expressions   <u>Medium:</u> Pencil

1 A smiling or laughing face looks round because of the cheeks. The mouth is turned upwards and the cheeks look smaller again because the cheeks are lifted.

2 With a sad expression the mouth and the eyes are turned down and the face looks longer.

3 The main feature in an angry expression are the eyebrows which are pointed towards the nose. The eyes are small and point down and the nostrils may be flared.

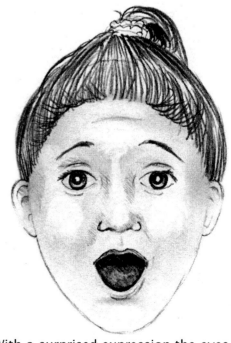

4 With a surprised expression the eyes look large, the eyebrows are raised and the mouth open making the face look longer.

People

Objectives   *To be able to draw a face in proportion.*
To be able to show different expressions.

Resources   Cartridge paper
HB, B and 2B pencils, rubbers

Activity   Remind the children how to draw a face with the guidelines as shown in 'People' Lesson 1. It is important to get the right shape/proportions for all of the following drawings.
Explain that faces change with different expressions.
It always works well to allow children to work with a partner and try out different faces. Encourage them to look at how the eyes/mouth/shape of the face change.

Extension   After initial sketches the activity could be extended to do a larger more detailed drawing in chalk or pastel.

5   When crying the eyes are almost closed and curved. The eyebrows point down and the mouth is open. Note the shape of the bottom lip and the added lines on the face.

6   For an evil grin look at the shape of the eyebrows raised at the outer edge and pointing down toward the nose. The mouth is a one sided smile.

Evaluation   Can you identify differnet expressions?
What makes them work?

Snapshot　　　　People 4

To use a skeletal structure to create the shape, and shading to create form.

To draw a person in proportion

<u>Medium:</u> Pencil

1 Draw an egg shape (4cm) for the head with a guideline from the chin down the page. Measure out the head length 5 more times down the line.

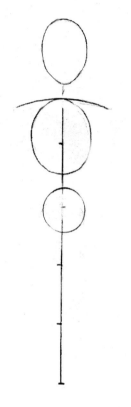

2 Leave a short space for the neck and draw the shoulders, about a head width either side of the line.
Draw an oval for the ribs and a circle for the pelvis.

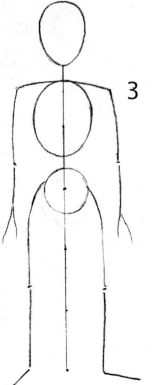

3 Draw the arms. The elbow lines up with the waist, the hands are between the hip and knee. Draw the legs. The knee is about halfway.

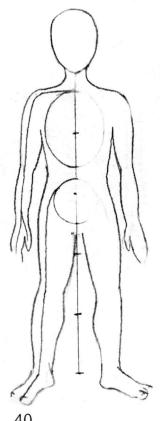

4 Now draw the body around the skeletal shape. The arms go in towards the elbow. The legs are wider at the thighs and thin towards the ankle.
Rub out all guidelines.

People

Objectives *To be able to draw a person using correct proportions.*

Resources Cartridge paper (A4)
HB, B and 2B pencils, rubbers

Activity To draw the body in proportion a 'skeletal structure' is used.
It is helpful to use a child as a model to compare proportions with the drawing, e.g. shoulder width, length of arms etc.

It is important to get the head the right size at the outset as it is then used to measure the rest of the body. On an A4 piece of paper this is about 4 cm. Obviously a larger piece of paper is needed for demonstrating to a whole class.

Once the marks have been measured out on the guide line use them to check the size of the other skeletal features.

5 Now details can be added. The face can be drawn as taught in 'People Lesson 1' Hair and clothing can be added.
Finally the drawing can be shaded to make it look 3D.

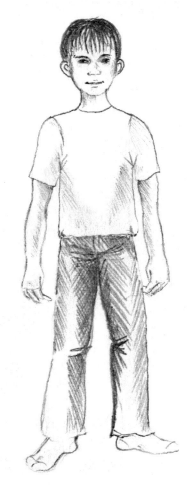

Evaluation Is the head the right size? Does the rest of the body look correctly proportioned?

Snapshot   People 5

To draw from close observation.

To draw a person in different poses

<u>Medium:</u> Charcoal

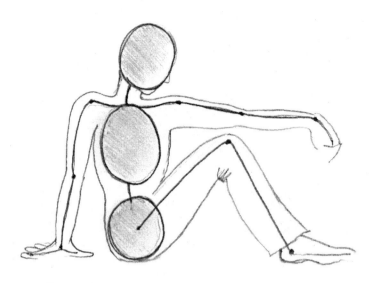

1 Draw out the skeletal structure to get the figure in the
   right position and in proportion. Once completed the
   body can be drawn around and details added.

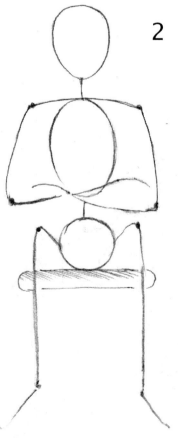

2 When the model is
   seated, note how
   the legs and feet
   are drawn to give
   the appearance
   of coming forwards.

People

Objectives *To be able to draw from observation.*
To draw different poses with correct proportions.

Resources Sugar paper (A3)
Charcoal or coloured chalks
Rubbers

Activity Children can work in pairs and model for one another.
They only need to model until the structure is drawn.
To help get the shape and the proportions it is best to lightly
draw in the skeletal structure as taught in 'People' Lesson 4. Once
the size and proportions are established the body can be drawn
around.

- A successful extension to this activity is to use work of well
known artists to copy from. There are many that feature whole
body poses.

3   Once children have gained some
confidence they can add more
details in terms of clothing,
expressions etc.

Evaluation Does the body look in proportion?
What improvements could be made?

43

Animals

Activity 1

Activity 2

Activity 3

Activity 4

Activity 5

Animals

Introduction

The following five lessons give step by step guides on how to draw animals. As with drawing people, the first two lessons focus on creating a frame, a skeletal structure as an aid to drawing in proportion.

It is worth encouraging children to do this at the start of each piece of work, as, not only does it help them to draw the right shapes, but also helps them to think about using the whole space available on the paper.

The next three lessons give the opportunity to try different materials and two of them are based on art from different cultures. They also provide the opportunity to work on a larger scale.

The larger projects can be worked on over two/three weeks completing the process in stages.

Snapshot   Animals 1

To use a skeletal structure to create the shape and marks to create texture and form.

How to draw cats and dogs   <u>Medium:</u> Pencil

1   Lightly draw the skeletal structure. Draw an oval for the head. Then draw a curve that goes diagonally down for the neck. Next draw a larger oval for the rib cage. Continue along with a horizontal line for the spine.
Draw a smaller circle at the end of the spine.

2   Draw in the front legs. They are straight. Draw in the back legs.
Look at the shape and where the joints are. Add on the tail.
Draw around the frame to create the body. Note the shape of the face.
Rub out the guidelines.

3   Draw in the eye and the nose.
Use marks to create the texture of fur and shading to make the body look 3D.
To create some perspective, areas in the background are shaded darker and those in the foreground lighter.

Animals

Objectives *To learn how to draw cats and dogs using a skeletal structure.*
To use marks to create form and texture.

Resources Cartridge paper A4/A3

Activity This could be separated into two lessons, but as the principles are the same they are included together.
As with drawing people the most important factor is to draw the skeletal structure first, whatever the pose.

To draw a dog follow exactly the same steps as for the cat.

1

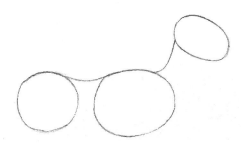

Note the shape of the head.
Demonstrate the different kinds of ears a dog could have.

2

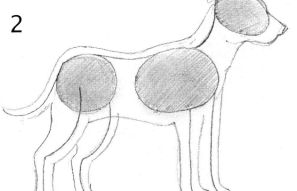

3

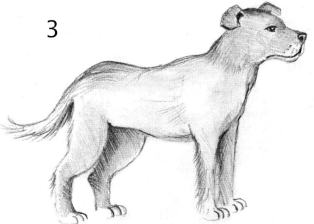

Evaluation Encourage children to share things that have worked well with their drawings.

49

To learn how to draw a horse using a skeletal structure.
To use curved/smudged marks to create form.

How to draw a horse   <u>Medium:</u> Charcoal/chalk

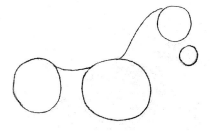

1   Lightly draw in the frame.
Draw 2 circles for the head, a smaller one for the nose. Draw a curve that goes diagonally down for the neck. Then draw a large oval for the rib cage. The spine curves down a little. For the rear end draw a circle slightly higher than the oval.

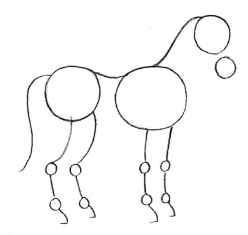

2   Draw the front legs. They are straight. Add 2 small circles for the joints and draw the hooves. Draw the back legs. Note where the joints are and where they bend.
Mark in the tail.

3   Now draw the body around the frame. Note how lines have been added to indicate muscles.
Draw the ears and the eye. The eye is quite high up. Draw in the nostrils and the mouth. Finally, add the mane.

Animals

Objectives *To learn how to draw a horse using a skeletal structure.*
To use curved/smudged marks to create form.

Resources Sugar paper (light colours) A3
Charcoal/dark grey chalk/brown chalk/ white chalk for highlights.

Activity As with other animals the best way to draw a horse so that it looks in proportion is to draw the skeletal structure first. This can be done lightly in charcoal or with an HB pencil.

4 Now use the charcoal or chalk to start shading in. If the marks are curved and smudged to follow the shape of the body, this helps to create form and a 3D effect.

Evaluation How has the drawing been successful? Are there parts that could be improved?

51

Snapshot   Animals 3

To look at work from different cultures and copy the style.

Drawing an Indian Elephant

<u>Medium:</u> Fabric pastels and paint
or oil pastels and paint

1

2

3

4

Animals

Objectives   *To look at art from other cultures and emulate the style.*
To explore different media.

Resources   White paper (A3/A2) HB and H pencil, rubbers
White calico
Fabric pastels/fabric paint
Oil pastels/watercolour paint (Use on cartridge paper)

Activity   To draw/paint an Indian Elephant on fabric (paper)

If working on paper as opposed to material eliminate tracing
process and use oil pastels to draw and watercolour to paint.

1.   On the white paper draw the skeletal structure of an elephant.
Draw around the body.

2.   Put the drawing under a piece of calico. Using a lighter H pencil
trace over the drawing on to the calico.

3.   Choose a fabric pastel (avoid black) and draw the outline.

4.   Choose another colour and draw the design on the body.

5.   Using fabric paints, paint in the shapes created by the design.
A limited colour range is more effective. Pearlised/metallic paints
work well with this activity.

5

Evaluation   Is the work similar in style to the artist's? Do the colours go well
together?

Snapshot   Animals 4

To look at work from different cultures and copy the style.

Drawing a Chinese Lion

Medium: Fabric pastels and paint
or oil pastels and paint

1

2

3

4

54

Animals

Objectives   *To look at art from other cultures and emulate the style.*
To explore different media.

Resources   White paper (A3/A2) HB and H pencils, rubbers
White calico
Fabric pastels/fabric paint
Oil pastels/water colour paint (Use on cartridge paper)

Activity   To draw/paint a Chinese Lion.
If working on paper as opposed to material eliminate tracing
process and use oil pastels to draw and watercolour to paint.

1. On white paper lightly draw out skeletal structure. Draw around
   the shape with an HB pencil.

2. Put the drawing under a piece of calico. Using a lighter H pencil
   trace over the drawing on to the calico.

3. Draw the outline with an oil pastel. To draw the mane use a range
   of colours with rapid dash marks.

4. Draw in the eyes, nose and mouth. The face is quite stylised, the
   eyes in particular. White pastel works well to make the teeth stand
   out.

5. Paint can now be added to complete the picture.
   If watercolours are used the colours can run into each other.

5

Evaluation   Is the style similar to the original picture?

To follow step by step instructions to complete a detailed picture.

Drawing a tiger's face   <u>Medium:</u> Water based paints.

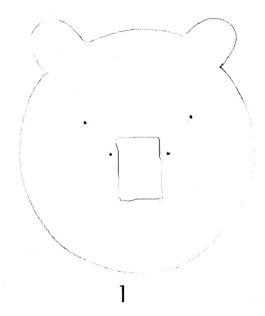

1

Draw a large circle filling most of the paper.
Draw in the ears. Draw 2 diagonal dots going in
towards the nose for each eye. Draw a rectangle
leaving enough space for the mouth and chin.

2

Using the dots draw in the eyes so that they are
slanted. Draw in the pupils. Note the shape. Draw a
T-shaped nose at the end of the rectangle. Draw in
the mouth and mark in the chin. Rub out the
rectangle.

3

Using yellow ochre and starting at the top paint
in areas of colour. Around the edges of the face
use brushstrokes to show the texture of the fur.

4

Whilst the paint dries paint the iris green leaving the
pupil for now. Mix a pink and paint the nose.

Animals

Objectives *To follow step by step instructions.*
To be able to match colours and patterns.

Resources Cartridge paper (A3)
HB pencils, rubbers.
Block paints: yellow ochre/black/green/red/white
Medium and fine brushes.

Activity To paint a tiger's face with detailed black markings.

For this activity instead of doing a demonstration the outcome is much more successful if led step by step.

Whenever adding black to a picture, it is always best to leave it to the end.

5

6

Using a thin brush and black paint begin to show the markings from the top of the head. The shapes are irregular. Work down section by section allowing children time to catch up.

Finally add the finishing touches. Paint in the pupils leaving a white dot to make the eyes shiny. A thin outline can be drawn around the nose and marks where the whiskers are around the mouth and chin.

Evaluation Which parts are successful.
Could any improvements be made?

57

Birds

Activity 1

Activity 2

Activity 3

Activity 4

Activity 5

Birds

Introduction

The following five lessons give step by step guides on how to draw birds. The first lesson shows how to draw the basic shapes and use marks to create a feathery texture. These basic principles can then be applied to further work.

The second lesson provides the opportunity to gather resources and research information to produce a detailed drawing. It is also a good colour matching exercise.

The next three lessons use different materials enabling children to practise and implement skills. The final lesson requires working in monochrome. The advantage of using only one colour is that the use of marks has to be carefully considered in order to differentiate between different textures.

Snapshot   Birds 1

Drawing in proportion and using marks to create texture and form.

How to draw a duck and a swan   Medium: Pencil

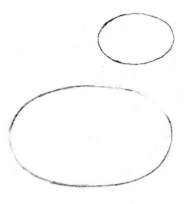

1 Draw 2 ovals, the larger one being level with the smaller one for the head.

2 Draw in the lines for the neck, the wings and the tail. Add in the eye and the beak.

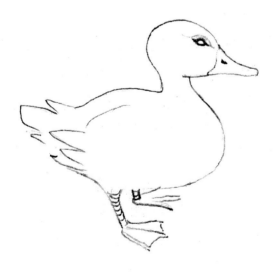

3 Draw in the legs and feet. Curved marks on the legs will make them look round.

4 Marks can now be added to show the feathers. If they are curved following the shape of the body they make it look 3D.

Birds

Objectives   *To be able to draw birds with head and body in proportion.
To use marks to create texture and form.*

Resources   Cartridge paper, HB pencils, rubbers.

Activity   To draw a duck and a swan looking at their different features.

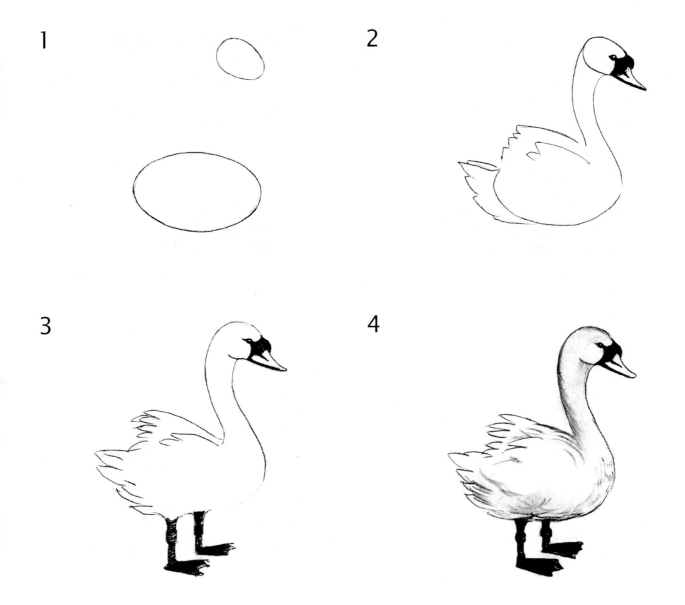

The steps for drawing a swan are almost the same as for the duck, except the two ovals are further apart to allow for the long neck. The legs are longer and thicker.

Evaluation   What are the differences between the duck and the swan?

Snapshot   Birds 2

Collecting visual images and sources of information to develop ideas.

Drawing birds from observation   Medium: pencil crayons/watercolour

1

2

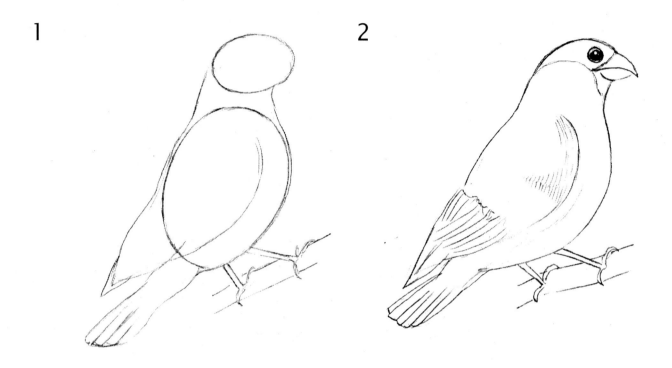

3

Birds

Objectives   *To use visual images to develop ideas e.g. reference books, Internet, photographs.*
To draw/paint birds matching shape and colour.

Resources   Reference books, photographs
Cartridge paper, HB pencils, rubbers
Colouring pencils/water soluble pencils/watercolours

Activity   To draw a bird form an image looking closely at shape, detail and colour.

1.   Select a photograph/image to work from.
Encourage children to identify the main shapes they can see.
Lightly draw out a circle for the head and the main shape of the body and if visible, wing, tail and legs.

2.   Draw around the shape more accurately looking at and referring to the image. Add in details of the eye, beak and lightly mark areas of colour/pattern on the bird.

3.   Demonstrate how to apply colour with a focus on:
   ▪ Creating form by the use of curved marks
   ▪ Creating form by the use of shading
   ▪ Creating texture by the use of marks

 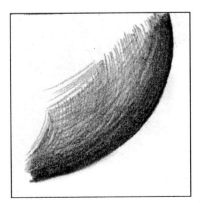 

Evaluation How does the finished drawing compare to the image in terms of shape/colour/detail?

Snapshot

Birds 3

To use marks to create pattern and texture using different tools.

To draw an owl in flight

Medium: Chalk

1

2

3

4

66

Birds

Objectives *To use marks to create pattern and texture using different tools.*
To recognise pattern and design in living things.

Resources Black/dark blue paper (A3)
White/brown/yellow/black carbon pencils/chalks
Rubbers

Activity To draw an owl in flight with a focus on the pattern and
symmetry of the wing feathers.

1.   Turn the paper so that it is landscape. Use thin white chalk.
     In the centre of the bottom quarter of the page, draw a circle for
     the head, and the body shape.
     Mark in the legs, feet and talons.

2.   From the top corner on each side draw the top of the wing.
     Draw in the main wing feathers.

3.   Draw in the other features. Point out the symmetry of the wings.
     Use white marks to show the details of the feathers. Use the
     brown chalk to add in extra detail.

4.   Draw the feathers around the eyes. Use the yellow to draw the
     eyes, beak, legs and feet. Use black to draw the talons and the
     pupils. Add white highlights.
     Use curved white marks to show the feathers on the head and
     body. Add a few brown flecks to complete the details.

Details of:

feathers   eyes   talons

 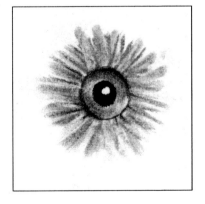 

Evaluation Do the wings look symmetrical. Can you see the pattern in the
feathers?

67

Snapshot   Birds 4

Use mixed media to create a reflection in water.

To draw a swan and its reflection   Medium: Oil pastel/wash

1

2

3

4

Birds

Objectives *To used mixed media.*
To apply drawing skills, using different tools.

Resources Cartridge paper (A3), HB pencils
Oil pastels, blue watercolour paint.

Activity To draw a swan and its reflection using mixed media.

1. Draw a light line halfway across the paper (landscape).
Using an HB pencil lightly draw the main shapes for the swan (as in 'Birds' Lesson 1) in the top half.

2. Turn the paper upside down and draw a mirror image in the bottom half. Draw the outline of both swans. Make the lines around the reflection wiggly. Now go over the outlines of both drawings with white oil pastel. Fill in the body of the swan with white pastel, fill in most of the reflection, also with white. Mark in a few feathers.

3. Draw in the eye and the beak.
Using brown and green pastels draw in some reeds in the top half, along the line. Turn the paper upside down and draw their reflections, making the lines wiggly.
Use blue and white oil pastel to draw some ripples around the swan.

4. Over the top half, use a watery blue wash to paint in the sky, painting over the reeds and the swan.
Use a slightly darker blue to paint over the reflection in the bottom half.

Evaluation Which parts are most successful?
Could any improvements be made?

69

Snapshot   Birds 5

To use different tools. To work in monochrome.
To use marks to record details.

Ink drawing of bird of prey   <u>Medium:</u> Pen and ink

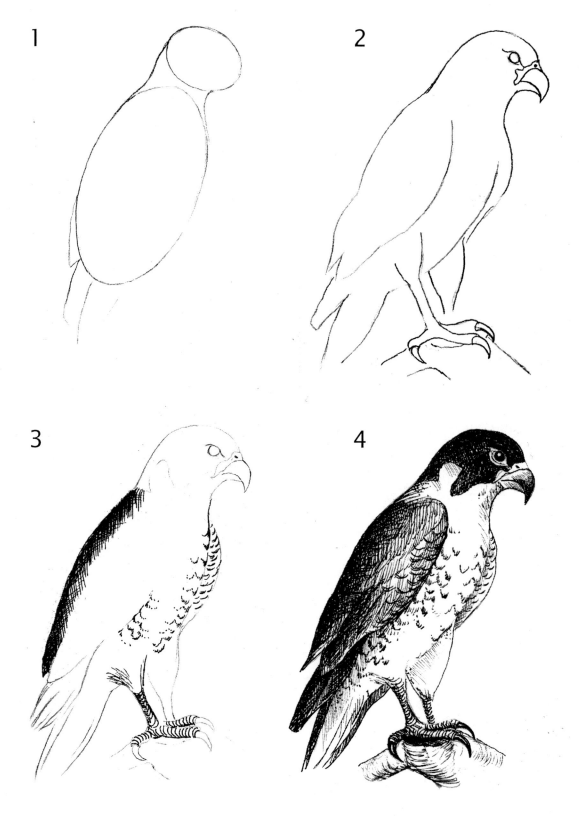

1

2

3

4

Birds

Objectives   *To use different tools. To work in monochrome.*
To use marks to record details.

Resources   Cartridge paper (A4)
HB pencils, rubbers
Pen and ink (fine tipped felt pens can be used)
Photographs of birds of prey

Activity   Bird of Prey in ink.

1. Lightly draw the oval shapes for the head and body using an HB pencil.

2. Draw the legs and mark in the eye, beak and talons.

3. Demonstrate how to dip the nib if using pen and ink.
   It is important to immerse the nib only, and not the holder as this leads to blots. Remind children to tap off excess ink.
   Begin to demonstrate how to apply marks, reinforcing that curved marks help to make the shape look round.
   Try out different marks for details of the feathers. Rings or bracelet shading can be used on the legs.

4. To add to the form, shading can be used by small dots or crosshatching. Remind the children to leave a white dot in the eye to make it look shiny. A white curve left on talons makes them look shiny too. The talons and the beak look effective if they are dark in contrast to the marks on the body.

Evaluation   Can you identify the bird? Which features make it recognisable?
Could any improvements be made?

Fish

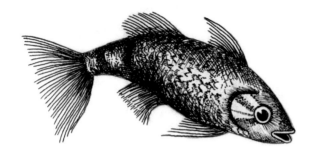

Activity 1

Activity 2

Activity 3

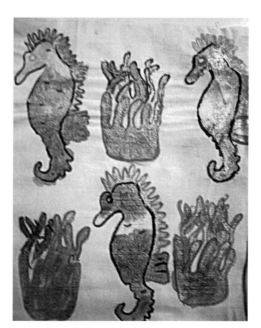

Activity 4

Fish

Introduction

The following four lessons allow the opportunity for more creative and imaginative work whilst reinforcing previously taught skills. Although each activity requires photos/images as a starting point, they are intended to stimulate ideas rather than be used as a basis for observational drawing as with previous activities.

The first lesson, as with other monochrome activities aims to refine mark making skills. What kind of marks create a scaly effect? How can you make something look scaly and 3D using only one colour?

The second lesson is ideal for encouraging collaborative work. For this to be successful children need to discuss the content of their picture, size and location of creatures and colours. Therefore they need to focus on all the key elements of making a good composition.
If the activity is carried out individually but on a large scale then it can be completed over two lessons.

The last two lessons are more design orientated and focus on colour and pattern. They also incorporate the use of different materials and can be more experimental.

Snapshot   Fish 1

To use pictures as a starting point to develop own ideas. To work in monochrome.

Medium: Pen/pen and ink

To draw a fish using marks in monochrome

1

2

3

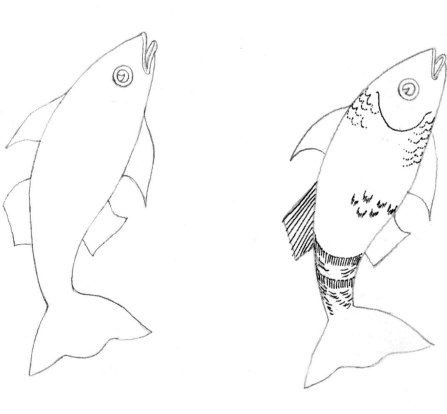

4

76

Fish

Objectives *To use different tools. To work in monochrome.*
To use pictures as a starting point to develop own ideas.

Resources Pictures of different kinds of fish
Cartridge/light coloured paper (A3/A4)
HB pencils, rubbers.
Either felt pens or pen and ink.

Activity To draw a fish, working in monochrome.
Look at a range of pictures. Discuss similarities and differences.
As part of the demonstration show how ideas can be taken from
different images and own imagination.

1. With an HB pencil draw the outline of a fish including tail and fins.
Mark in the eye.

2. Remind children how to make a variety of marks.
Explain the picture is going to be monochrome, that is, using only
one colour. If pen and ink is used show how to dip the pen and
make marks.
It is important to immerse the nib only, and not the holder as this
leads to blots. Remind children to tap off excess ink.

3. Begin to apply marks, reinforcing that if marks are curved, it helps
to make the shape look 3D. Use a variety of different marks.

4. Show how shading can be added by the use of dots, or cross
hatching. Complete the eye, remembering to leave a white spot to
make the eye look shiny.

Evaluation Have a variety of different marks been used? Does the fish look
3D? How was that achieved?

Snapshot   Fish 2

To use images and own imagination to make a composition, thinking about shape and space.

Drawing an Underwater sea picture   <u>Medium:</u> Oil pastel and wash

1

2

3

4

Fish

Objectives *To create a composition based on images and own imagination.*
To consider shape and space.

Resources Cartridge paper (A3/A2)
HB pencils
Oil pastels, blue wash (watery ready-mix/watercolour)
Images of sea creatures: fish/jellyfish/sea horses etc.

Activity This activity can be worked on in pairs.
To create an underwater sea picture.
Show children a range of pictures of different sea creatures.
Explain how we can use these to give us ideas but can use our
own imagination.

1. Use a large piece of paper. Using a pencil begin to draw shapes of
    different creatures. Talk about the shapes and spaces so that the
    picture looks balanced.

2. Draw over the shape using different colour pastels.
    The pastel marks need to be firm to show through the wash.
    Once the outlines have been done, details of scales, fins etc. can
    be added but, these should be in the form of marks, and NOT
    coloured in.

3. Add in some seaweed/coral/rocks at the bottom of the paper.
    Blue and white pastel lines can be added to show
    movement/waves in the water.

4. Once the pastel marks are completed wash over the whole picture
    with a thick brush. It is well worth testing the wash before
    applying. If it is too thick the pastel won't show through. If it is
    too thin the colour will be insipid.

Evaluation Are the shapes of the sea creatures well spaced out ?
Are the colours bright enough so they show through well?

Snapshot   Fish 3

To use different tools and techniques.

Drawing a metallic seahorse   <u>Medium:</u> Metallic paints.

1

2

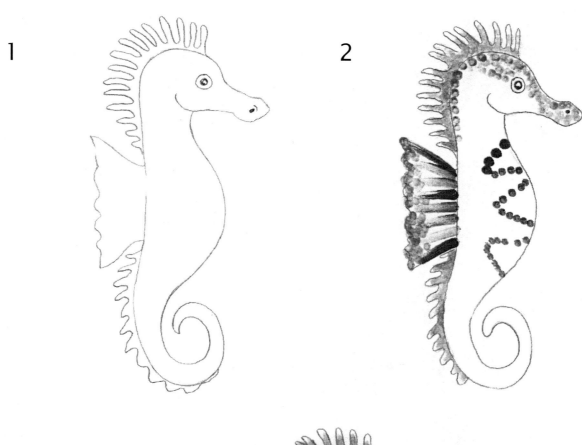

3

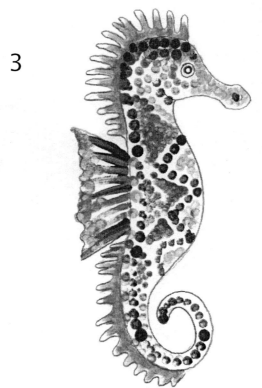

Fish

Objectives *To use different tools and techniques to create an image.*
To consider the use of colour and pattern.

Resources Black paper (A4)
HB pencils, rubbers
Metallic paints, cotton buds

Activity To make a dotty metallic seahorse.

1. Draw the outline of a seahorse in pencil.

2. Encourage the children to think about the colours they will use
    and about creating a pattern. Discuss colours that go together
    well, or maybe only using 3 colours in total. This encourages
    them to think more about the overall pattern.
    Demonstrate how to apply the colour using the cotton bud and
    dots.

3. Show examples of how different patterns can be made.

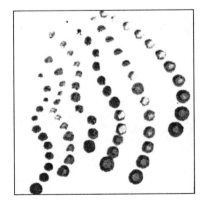 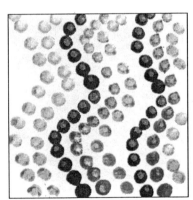 

Evaluation Do the colours go together well?
Are there different patterns in the picture?

81

Snapshot   Fish 4

To use different tools and techniques. To create a repeated pattern.

Sea creatures on fabric   <u>Medium:</u> Fabric pastels/paints

1

2

3

4

Fish

Objectives   *To use different tools and techniques.*
To create a repeated pattern.

Resources   Cartridge paper (A5)
HB/H pencils, rubbers
White calico (A4 pieces minimum)
Fabric pastels/paints, fabric dye
Reference books/photos

Activity   To make a repeated pattern of sea creatures on fabric.

1.   Using images for reference select two different creatures.
Fold the A5 paper in half and draw an outline for each one on either half of the paper. (Stencils can be used for very young children)

2.   Lay the material over the paper. Use an H pencil and begin at the top left corner alternating the pictures until all the material is covered. Demonstrate how to space the pictures out so that an even pattern is created.

3.   Once the material has been filled with the pencil designs draw over them with pastels.

4.   Once all the pencil has been covered with pastel each picture can then be painted with fabric paints. Finally the background can be filled in. It is easier to use a dye to complete the larger spaces.

Ironing over the top of the fabric seals the colour.

Evaluation   Are the pictures in the right order?
Are the spaces between the pictures the same?

Flowers

Activity 1

Activity 2

Activity 3

Activity 4

Flowers

Introduction

The following four lessons provide activities for drawing flowers.
The first two are very much based on observation. Often children draw flowers and plants with very thick stems and are surprised to observe how thin they really are.

It is amazing how even very young children can accurately represent what they see, when their attention is focused on details and a step by step approach is taken to teach them.

A key aim is to consider how to apply marks that convey the delicacy of petals. The lessons also look at the application of colour using different materials.

The next two lessons are more design based and use flowers to create a repeated pattern. They also provide the opportunity to try out different tools and materials.

Snapshot   Flowers 1

To draw from observation. To use marks and lines to communicate the delicacy of the petals.

Drawing flowers   Medium: Chalks

1

2

3

4

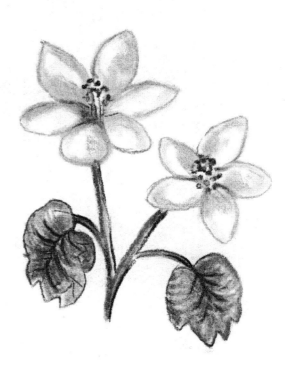

Flowers

Objectives *To draw from observation.*
To use lines and marks to communicate the delicacy of the petals.

Resources Variety of different flowers
Black paper (A4/A3)
Chalks, cotton buds.

Activity To draw and colour flowers in chalk.

1. Choose an example to draw. Discuss the shape of the flowers, stem and leaves. Look particularly at the shapes of the petals. Explain that the marks used need to be light and soft because the petals are delicate.
Using the appropriate colour lightly draw in the line of the stem making sure it is thin.

2. Lightly mark in where the individual flowers and leaves are going to go. Demonstrate how to colour in the petals blending light and dark of the same colour to give some form. Cotton buds are useful for blending colours together.

3. The leaves can be drawn and coloured in the same way.
Using different greens and yellow add to their appearance.

4. Final details can be added such as veins on leaves and highlights on petals can be added.
Any unwanted smudges can be rubbed out.

Evaluation Can you identify which flower it is?
Do the petals look soft and delicate? How has this been achieved?

Snapshot   Flowers 2

To draw from observation. To look closely at colours and match them.

Paintings flowers   <u>Medium:</u> Watercolour

1

2

3

4

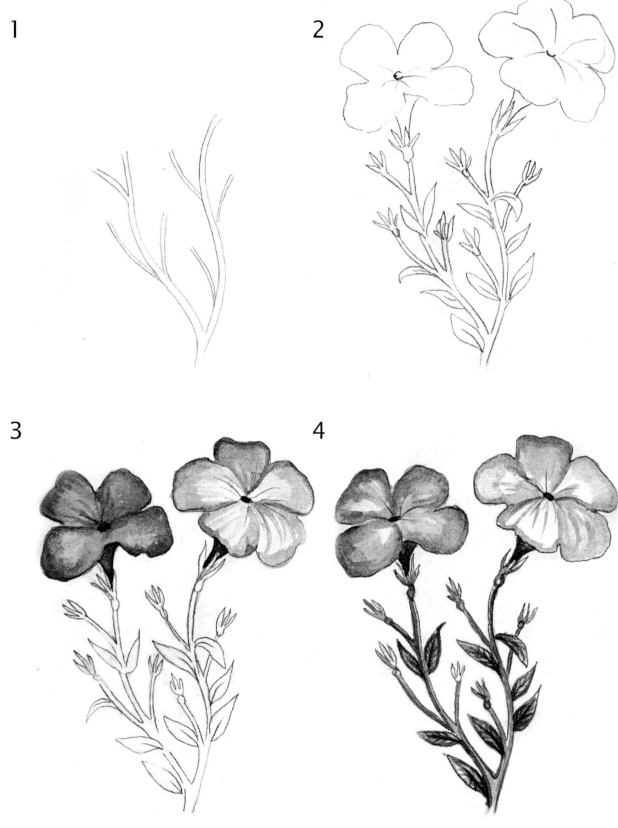

Flowers

Objectives *To draw from observation.*
To look closely at colours and match them.

Resources Variety of flowers
Cartridge paper (A4/A3)
HB pencils, rubbers
Watercolour brushes and paints.

Activity To paint flowers in watercolour.

1. Choose an example to draw. Discuss the shape of the flowers,
    stem and leaves. Look particularly at the shapes of the petals.
    Explain that the marks used need to be light and soft because the
    petals are delicate.
    Using an HB pencil lightly mark out the line of the stem.

2. Lightly draw the outline of the petals and the leaves.

3. Demonstrate how to use watercolour paints. Show how water is
    used to make colours paler and how the colours can be allowed
    to run into one another. For a deeper colour more paint can be
    added on top of an existing coat.
    Begin with the petals. Start at the outer edge of each petal and
    add water to lighten the colour towards the centre.
    Other colours can be added whilst the paint is wet.

4. To paint the leaves use lighter and darker green.
    Colour can be lifted out with a tissue to create a varied effect.
    Any unwanted pencil marks can be removed once the paint is
    completely dry.

Evaluation Do the colours match the real flower? Are the shapes of the petals
the same? Do the petals look soft ?

Snapshot   Flowers 3

To use different materials and processes.
To create a repeated pattern.

Floral design   Medium: Fabric pastel/paints

1

2

3

4

Flowers

Objectives *To use different materials and processes.*
To create a floral design with a repeated pattern.

Resources Reference materials of flowers fabric designs
Small squares of white paper (10 cm minimum)
HB and H pencils, rubbers
White calico
Fabric pastels/paints, fabric dye

Activity To create a floral design on fabric with a repeated pattern.

1. On the small white paper draw out a flower using an HB pencil.
    This can be done as a very simple design, or for older children as
    a more complicated design with more detail and leaves.

2. Place the design under the material in the top left hand corner.
    Trace over the drawing carefully with an H pencil.
    Demonstrate how to repeat the image making sure the spacing is
    even. Continue to the bottom right hand corner.

3. Now draw around each flower with fabric pastels. They can all be
    identical or colours can alternate but emphasise the importance of
    maintaining a pattern.

4. Once all the pastel is complete, the flowers can be painted with
    fabric paints. The colours can be blended.
    The background can then be completed with fabric dye.

Evaluation Is the pattern maintained over the whole piece?
Has the design been evenly spaced out?

93

Snapshot   Flowers 4

To use different tools and techniques.
To create a repeated pattern.

Flower Prints   <u>Medium:</u> Printing inks

1

2

3

4

94

Flowers

Objectives *To use different tools and techniques*
Use own work as a starting point for applying skills to a different media.

Resources Examples of previous work on flowers.
Small pieces of white paper. Larger paper for printing.
HB pencils, rubbers.
Polystyrene printing tiles cut into squares (10 cm minimum)
Printing inks/rollers/trays.

Activity To print flower designs.

1. On the small piece of paper draw out a simple design for a flower. Add some marks or dots to add to the design as these print well.

2. Check the designs are large enough and clear enough.
When they are, the design can be copied onto the polystyrene tile. This is done by drawing with a pencil.
The marks need to be firm enough to make an indent in the tile otherwise it won't print.

3. Once the tile is ready a roller is used to transfer ink on to it. The tile is then placed face down on to the final paper carefully and rubbed on the back. It needs to be lifted off carefully too.

4. More prints can be carried out and a range of colours tried. Encourage the children to think about spacing their prints evenly across the page.

For the printing to be successful, the ink needs to be rolled evenly over the tile and must not be too thick! The marks in the tile also need to be deep enough for a successful outcome.

Evaluation Has the printing come out clearly? Can you think of any reasons why it may not have worked so well?

Trees

Activity 1

Activity 2

Activity 3

Activity 4

Trees

Introduction

Beyond a 'lollypop stick tree', trees can be quite hard to draw.
The following four lessons look at how to draw a basic shape, then how to apply different techniques to represent the bark and the foliage.

The first lesson gives a step by step guide using pencil. Some children find it quite hard to divide the branches so it is well worth differentiating this activity and where necessary simply dividing the trunk into two branches with maybe one other line of branches after that.
It is also worth pointing out that leaves grow on the higher branches and not all the way down the trunk. It may sound obvious but children often draw leaves on the trunk if it is not pointed out.

The first two lessons are very good for reinforcing mark making skills, thinking about the most effective marks for representing both leaves and bark.

The last two lessons allow the opportunity for more creativity and expression.
For lesson four, if natural sponge is available it is very effective for both leaves and blossom.
This activity has been very successful with young children, the combination of scratching paint off on the trunk and dabbing the sponges make it a favourite.

Snapshot   Trees 1

To learn how to draw a tree with branches and foliage.

To draw a tree in detail   Medium: Pencil

1

2

3

4

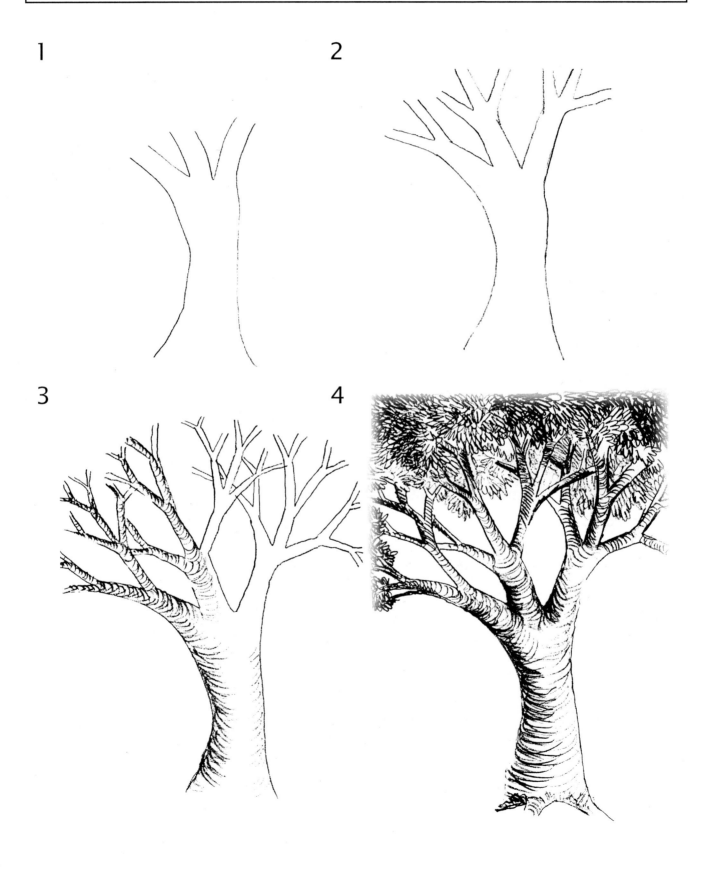

Trees

Objectives *To learn how to draw a tree with branches and foliage.*
To use bracelet shading and appropriate marks.

Resources Cartridge paper (A4/A3)
HB, B and 2B pencils, rubbers
Pictures of trees

Activity A pencil drawing of a tree.

1. In the bottom half of the paper draw the trunk (not too wide) with
3 main branches using an HB pencil.
To simplify for younger children divide trunk into 2 branches and
only divide once more.

2. Now divide each of these three branches into 2/3 thinner ones.

3. Continue to divide each of these, moving outwards on the page
until finally the branches have become twigs.
Apply some bracelet shading to create the round effect of the
trunk and branches. Try different grades of pencils.

4. The leaves are then added by mark making. More shading can be
added to enhance the 3D effect. Also shading some leaves helps
create perspective. Bolder lines come forward, fainter lines recede.

Details of marks used.

Bracelet shading   Leaves   Shading of leaves

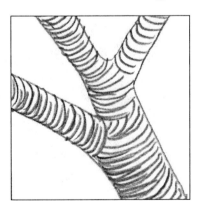

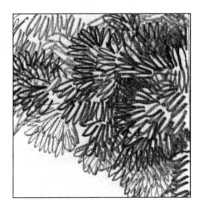

Evaluation Does the tree look in proportion? Does the trunk look round?

Snapshot   Trees 2

To use different tools. To use marks to communicate meaning.

To draw a tree in monochrome   Medium: Pen and ink

1

2

3

4

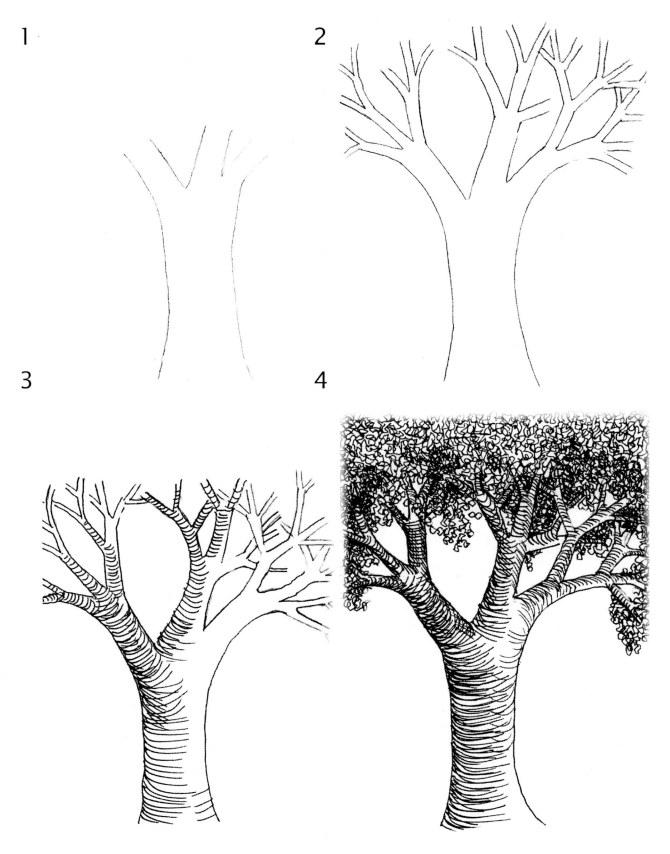

Trees

Objectives To use different tools. To use marks to communicate meaning and visually describe ideas.

Resources Cartridge paper (A4)
HB pencils, rubbers
Pen and ink (felt pens can be used with younger children)

Activity To draw a tree in pen and ink.

1. In the bottom half of the paper draw the trunk with three main branches using an HB pencil.

2. Now divide each of these three branches into 2/3 thinner ones. Continue to divide each of these, moving outwards on the page until finally the branches have become twigs.

3. On a separate piece of paper demonstrate how to dip the nib and make marks with the ink. It is important to immerse the nib only, and not the holder as this leads to blots. Remind children to tap off excess ink.
Begin to apply marks to the tree beginning with bracelet shading as in 'Trees Lesson 1.'

4. Make marks to represent the leaves. To complete the picture remind the children about crosshatching and dots as a way of shading when working in monochrome.

Details of marks used.

Bracelet shading   Leaves   Shading of leaves
crosshatching

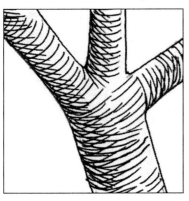

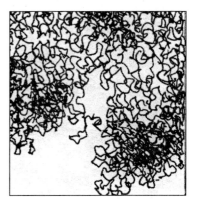

Evaluation Have the appropriate marks been used to create the right effect?

Snapshot   Trees 3

To apply skills and knowledge to different processes.

A blossom tree in chalk   <u>Medium:</u> Chalk

1

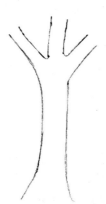

2

3

4

Trees

Objectives To apply skills and knowledge to different processes.
To use own work as a starting point to develop new ideas.

Resources Pencil drawings of trees (as reference)
Black paper (A3)
HB pencils, rubbers
Chalks
Cotton buds

Activity To draw a blossom tree in chalk.

Use children's own drawings of trees as a starting point and reminder of the process.

1. In the bottom half of the paper draw the trunk with three main branches using an HB pencil.

2. Now divide each of these three branches into 2/3 thinner ones. Continue to divide each of these, moving outwards on the page until finally the branches have become twigs.

3. Using different tones of brown or grey chalks make curved marks to create the trunk. Darker colours around the edge and lighter colours in the centre help enhance the 3D effect.

4. Using a range of pinks/white begin making marks for the blossom using the darker colours first and using the lighter colours and white as highlights.
Do not completely fill the whole area but work around the branches so that the shape of the tree is not lost.
Cotton buds can be used to blend colours. Rubbers can be used to redefine shapes if they have been lost and also to clean any unwanted smudges.

Evaluation Which parts of the picture have worked well?
Are there any parts that could be improved?

To investigate the possibilities of different tools and materials.

To print a tree using sponges   <u>Medium:</u> Paint and sponges

1

2

3

4

Trees

Objectives   *To investigate the possibilities of different tools and materials.*
To apply skills to different techniques.

Resources   Cartridge/light coloured paper (A3/A2)
HB pencils, rubbers
Sponge markers, small sponges (natural), plastic forks.
Thick paint: range of browns/greens/pinks (for blossom)

Activity   To print a tree using sponge.

1.   In the bottom half of the paper draw the trunk with three main branches using an HB pencil.

2.   Now divide each of these three branches into three thinner ones. Continue to divide each of these, moving outwards on the page until finally the branches have become twigs.

3.   Using the sponge markers begin to sponge paint on the trunk and branches. Curve the marks and apply darker colours around the edges and lighter in the middle to help create a round shape. As the branches become thinner paint one colour but add a lighter colour along the top edge again to help create some form. Whilst the paint is wet use the plastic forks to scratch off some paint. Curve the marks. It creates a great woody texture.

4.   Using the natural sponge and starting with a dark green begin to sponge areas of colour along the branches. Gradually work through the shades of green finishing with the lightest to create highlights.

Evaluation   Were the sponges easy to work with?
Did they create the effect you wanted?

Landscapes

Activity 1

Activity 2

Activity 3

Landscapes

Introduction

The following three lessons provide the opportunity to try some
landscapes using different processes.
The first lesson is very simple and the main aim is to teach how the use of
colour helps create perspective. The lighter tone of a colour recedes and the
darker tone comes forward.

The second lesson uses the work of Van Gogh as a starting point
and encourages children to think about applying the materials in a certain
style. There are many other landscapes of his that could be used equally
successfully, following the same steps.
The choice of materials has been left open. All work well, it is really a matter of
preference, and practicality.

Lesson 3 allows for exploration of different tools and the chance to discover
their effect on the paint. Encourage children to come up with their own ideas
and to be as creative as they can with the use of tools.
Different ideas can be demonstrated on the same area, e.g. on the grass, or the
water.
The activity generates useful discussion amongst the children about
how they created certain effects and so is well worth expanding on in the
evaluation as it is provides practical knowledge for future work.

Snapshot   Landscapes 1

To create perspective using tones of colour. To learn that lighter colours recede and darker colours come forward.

Landscape of mountains   <u>Medium:</u> Paint

1

2

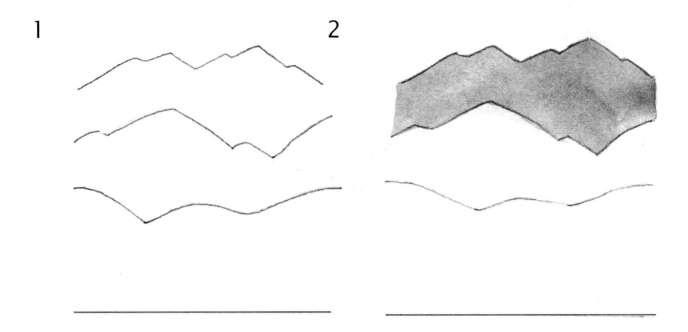

3

4

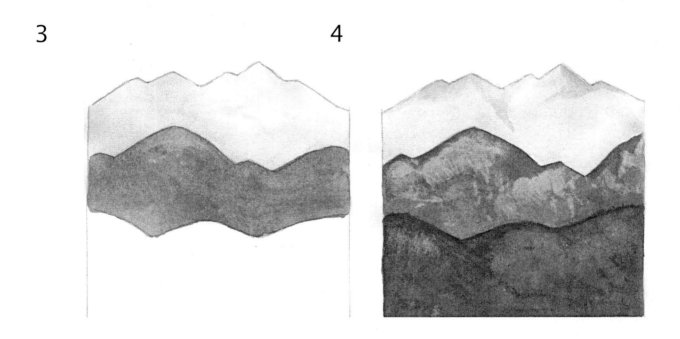

Landscapes

Objectives   *To create perspective using tones of colour.*
To learn that lighter colours recede and darker colours come forward.

Resources   Cartridge paper (A3)
HB pencils, rubbers
Readymix/poster paint – one colour and white

Activity   Landscape of mountains.

Explain that the activity is about creating perspective.
The mountains in the distance will look lighter/fainter, and those in the foreground darker and nearer.
Demonstrate how to mix the paint. Start with a colour (black/blue/purple) in its neat state, it will be the darkest.
For the second tone add half colour/half white. For the third tone, mainly white with a small dash of the colour.

1.   A quarter of the way down the page draw the first line of mountains, simply an irregular zig-zag line with an HB pencil. About halfway down draw the next line of mountains so that the peaks are in different places to the first line. Finally draw the mountains in the foreground.

2.   Starting with the lightest colour paint the first line of mountains, in the background.

3.   Using the middle tone, paint the middle line of mountains.

4.   With the darker tone paint the mountains in the foreground. To add more details subtle, slightly darker lines can be added to each line to add form. Or, small areas of colour can be lifted out of peaks by brushing some water into a small area and lifting paint out with a paper towel.

Evaluation   Does the picture have perspective? Why do the mountains in the background look more distant?

Snapshot   Landscapes 2

To create own landscape based on the style of a well known artist.
To match colour and use of marks.

Copy of landscape by Van Gogh

<u>Medium:</u> pastels/paint

1

2

3

4

Landscapes

Objectives *To create own work in the style of a well known artist.*
To match colour and use of marks.

Resources Cartridge paper (A4/A3)
HB pencils, rubbers
Either chalk pastels/paints/oil pastels
Copies of landscapes by Van Gogh

Activity To draw a landscape in the style of Van Gogh.

For this activity, any of the suggested media work well. Chalks are probably the easiest in terms of colour matching and applying marks but they do smudge.
With chalks always work down the page and leave darker colours until the end.

1. Mark the sky line and draw out the main shapes in pencil.

2. Beginning with the sky select the colours to match the original and demonstrate how to make marks in the same way as the artist.

3. Start to work along the horizon matching the colours, shapes and marks. Work towards the foreground adding in overall colour and shapes maintaining the kind of marks used by the artist.

4. Add final details and marks looking closely at the artist's work. If using chalk add the final darker colours at the end.

Evaluation How is the picture similar to the artist's?
Are some parts different? Why do you think that is?

115

Snapshot   Landscapes 3

To create a landscape using ideas and techniques from previous activities.
To use a variety of materials.

Medium: Paint

Landscape based on printing techniques

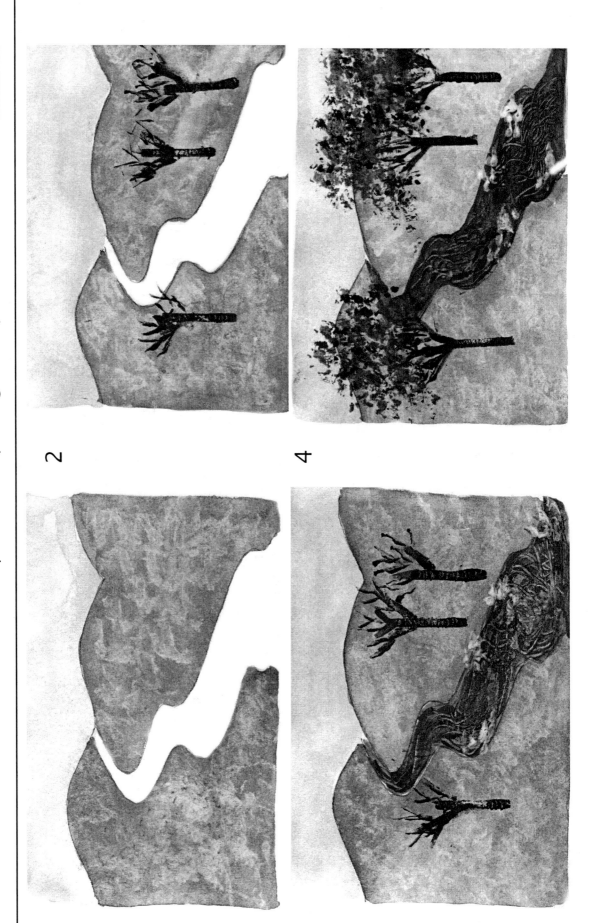

1

2

3

4

Landscapes

Objectives   To create landscape using ideas and techniques from previous activities.
To use printing techniques.

Resources   Light blue paper (A3/A2)
HB pencils, rubbers
Paints (block/readymix): greens/browns/reds/pinks
Sponges (natural)
Plastic forks, range of mark making tools, pieces of card

Activity   Landscape using printing techniques.

A specific example is given here but encourage children to create their own landscape.

1.   Using the HB pencil draw a line of hills. Show how a river could be added along the bottom or diagonally across the page. Paint the hills and sky with block paints; these dry quickly. Whilst the hills are wet, experiment printing with different tools to create a grassy texture.

2.   Using the edge of the card print vertical lines to make tree trunks. Sponge a lighter brown on to the trunk to fill in the colour. Use a fork to scratch patterns into the trunk creating the effect of bark. This needs to be done whilst the paint is wet.

3.   Paint the water with readymix paint. Try different tools to show the water surface. Splashes can be added with sponges.

4.   Beginning with the crimson and some natural sponge, dab some colour on the branches to create blossom. Add lighter colours to give depth to the trees.

Evaluation   Which tools worked well for making marks?
Could they have been used differently?

117

Water

Activity 1

Activity 2

Activity 3

Water

Introduction

The following three lessons provide different ways of looking at how to draw/paint water. The first two lessons focus on the movement and energy and the last one on the reflective quality of water.

The success of Lesson 1 relies on the marks being applied vigorously to create the effect of the water crashing down the rocks. It is important that the oil pastels are applied firmly for them to show through the wash. The wash needs to be quite watery to create the desired effect.

In Lesson 2 a specific Monet picture has been chosen as an example, but he painted several in a similar style. The one selected has a simple composition. Some others are:

- Rough Sea
- Rough Sea at Etretat
- Sea at Fecamp
- The Wild Sea

Lesson 3 shows how to create a reflection on water with chalks, as they are the easiest medium to use. The activity could be followed up by using paint as an extension. Pictures of sunsets are easily available in calendars/books etc.

Snapshot   Water 1

To work from own imagination. To create movement and energy by the way the marks are applied.

To create a waterfall using mixed media   Medium: Oil pastel/wash

1

2

3

4

Water

Objectives *To work from own imagination to create movement in water. To use mixed media to create the desired effect.*

Resources Cartridge paper (A3)
Oil pastels, watercolour paints
White readymix/poster paint, sponge (natural)
Pictures of waterfalls/gushing water

Activity A gushing waterfall using mixed media.

The main objective is to create a picture with movement and energy so the marks for the water need to be applied with vigour!

1. Using grey pastels mark out the shape of rocks down the page. Using greens and browns, some bushes/trees can be added. Add some detail to give some form but avoid completely colouring in.

2. Using vigorous marks down the page do swirls and lines in white, pastel and different blues.

3. Use watercolour washes of grey to go over the rocks and greens and browns for any foliage. Start with a light blue wash and downward movements on the waterfall. Slightly darken the blue with more paint and add some lines of darker blue into the water.

4. Allow a few minutes for the wash to dry. Then, using thicker white paint, dab splashes on with the sponge.

Evaluation Does the water look like it is crashing down the rocks?
Is there movement in the picture, how was this achieved?

Snapshot   Water 2

To use different tools to create a desired effect.
To use the work of a famous artist as a starting point.

Medium: Paint

A seascape with waves

1

2

3

4

Water

Objectives *To use different tools to create a desired effect.*
To use the work of a famous artist as a starting point.

Resources Cartridge paper (A3/A2)
Readymix/poster paints
Thick brushes, tools for scraping (plastic forks)
Monet sea pictures e.g.'Rough Sea'

Activity A seascape with waves.

There are several appropriate sea pictures by Monet.
Select one and discuss how he used his brush marks to create the waves.

1. Just above halfway, mark a horizontal line across the page as the horizon. Using different light blues demonstrate how to apply marks on the sky in the style of the artist.

2. Using darker blues create the waves with curved 'C' shaped colours by mixing blues/greens.

3. The whole picture can be completed in the style of the artist, or, to add to the effect, marks can be scraped with a fork whilst the paint is still wet.
    This technique is called 'scraffito'.

4. Once the sea and sky have been completed, use a hard bristled brush (an old toothbrush is ideal) to spray some white paint on the edges of some of the waves to create foam.

Evaluation Has the picture captured some of the style of the artist? How has this been done? Is there movement in the waves?

Snapshot   Water 3   To create light reflecting on water using knowledge and understanding of materials.

Medium: Chalks

The sun reflected on water

1

2

3

4

126

Water

Objectives To create light reflecting on water using knowledge and understanding of materials.
To be selective with use of colour.

Resources Cartridge paper (A3)
Rubbers, chalks: reds/oranges/yellows
A circular object to draw around, cotton buds.

Activity Chalk drawing of sun reflecting on water.

1. Use a light chalk and about half way down the page draw a horizontal line as the horizon. In the centre of the sky draw around a circular object (about 6cm diameter).

2. Leave the circle white. Around it, using the flat side of the chalk begin with a yellow from the edge of the sun and then working outwards blend in orange and reds towards the outer edge of the paper and down to the horizon.

3. From the centre of the horizon under the sun, draw 2 lines that widen as they come towards the foreground.
This is to mark where the light reflects and helps to create perspective.

4. Using similar colours to the sky make horizontal wavy marks to create the surface of the water, leaving the space between the two lines white. Blend some of these lines but maintain the wavy effect.
Finally add a tiny bit of colour to the sun, and using the paler colours add a few wavy marks into the reflection.

Evaluation Does the sun look like it is reflecting on the water?
Does the picture have perspective?

127

Still Life - Lesson 3

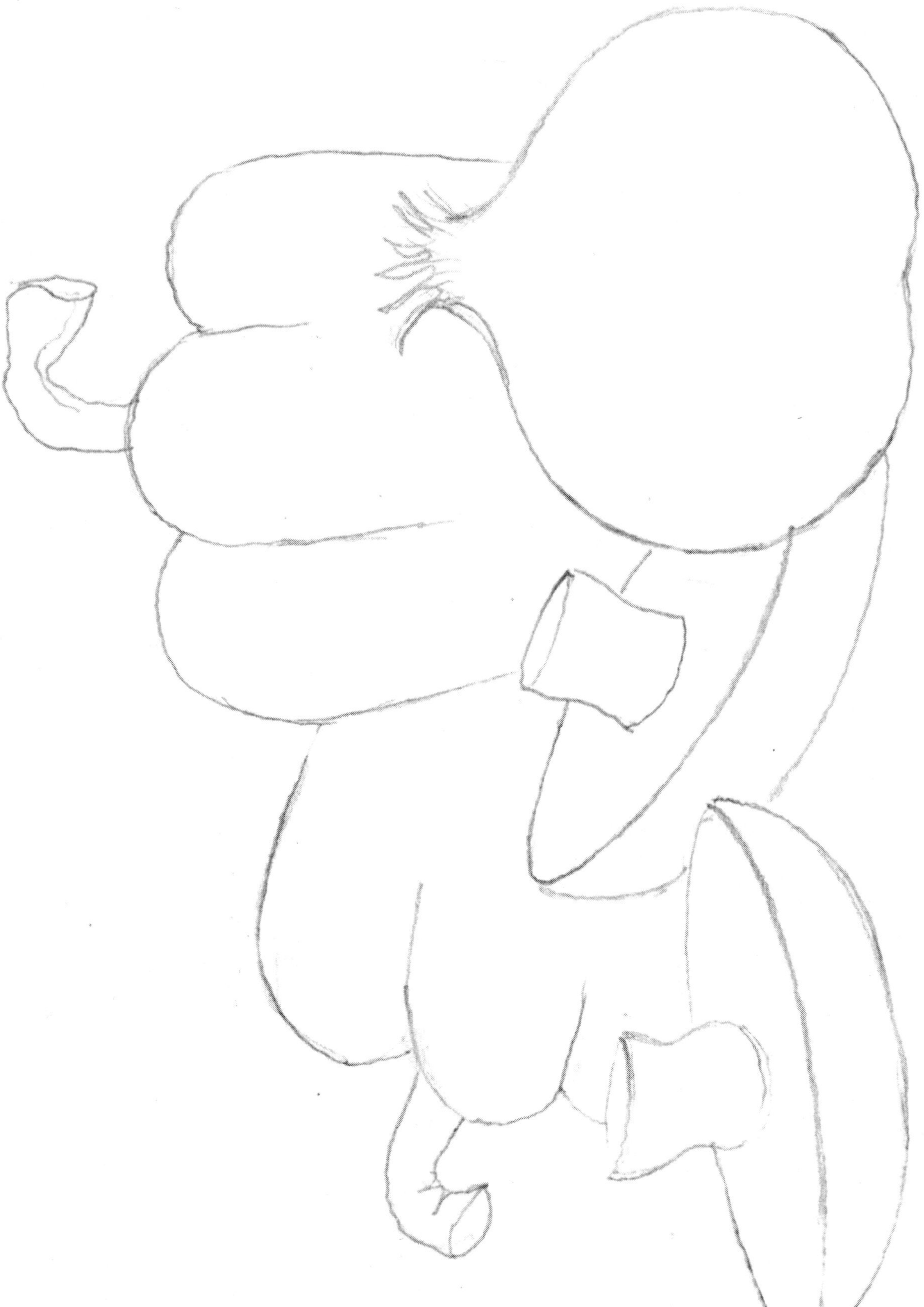

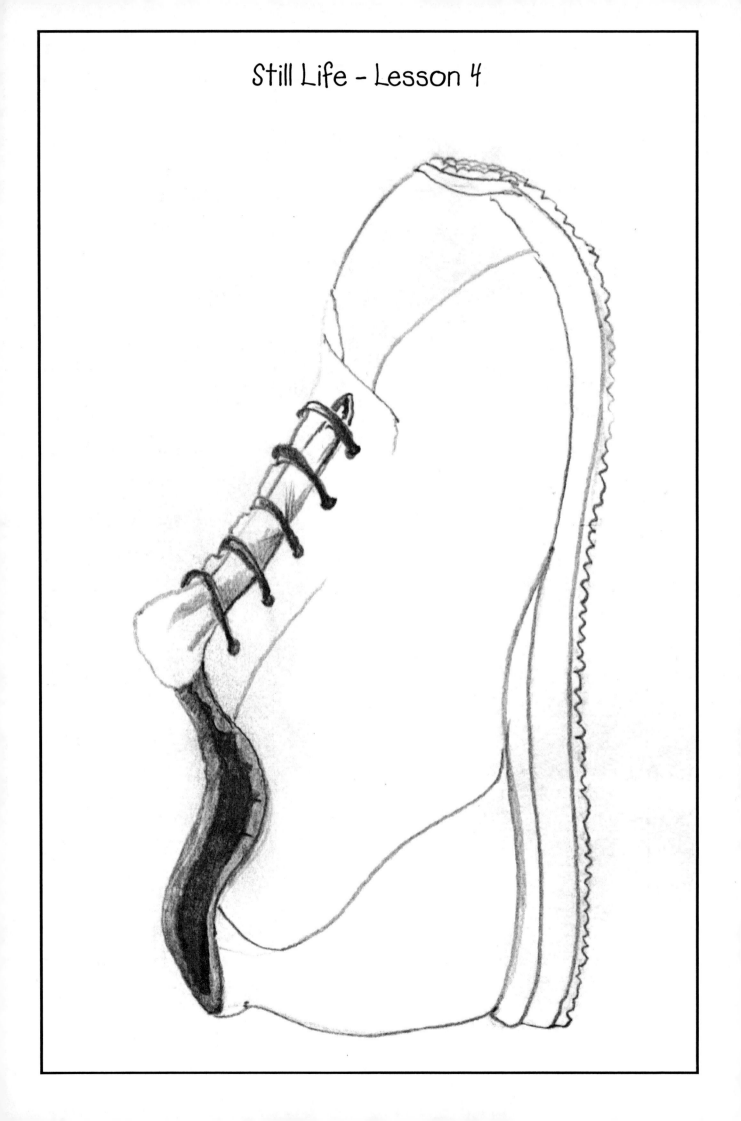

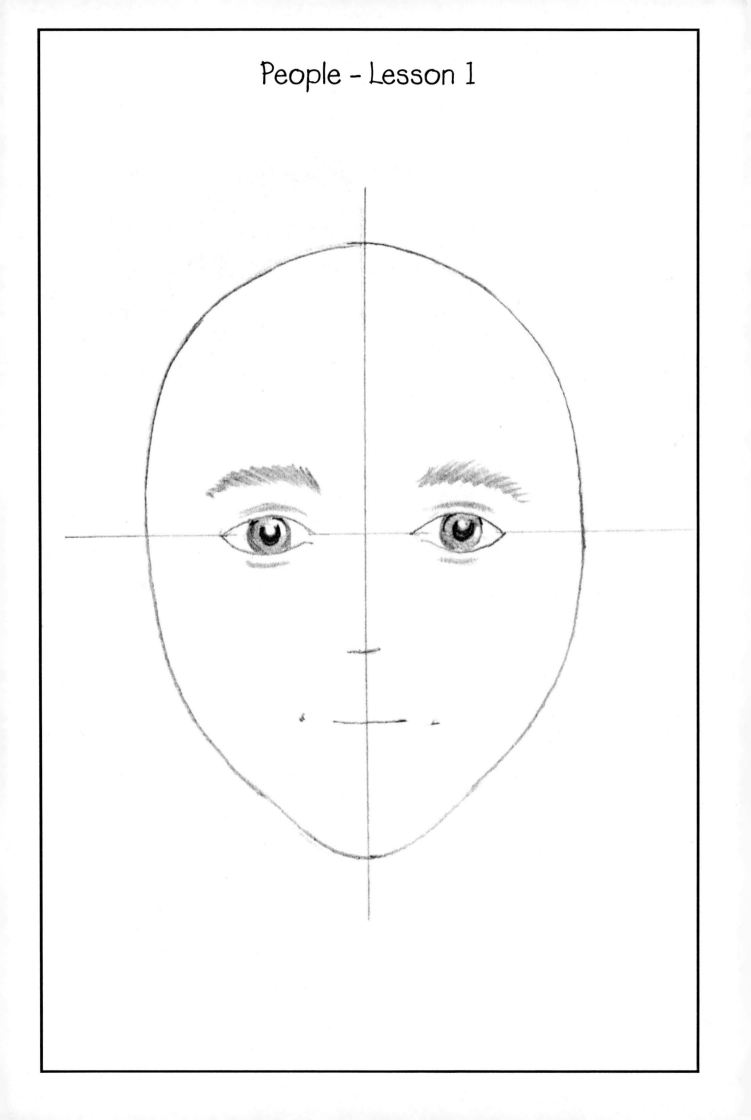

Animals - Lesson 2

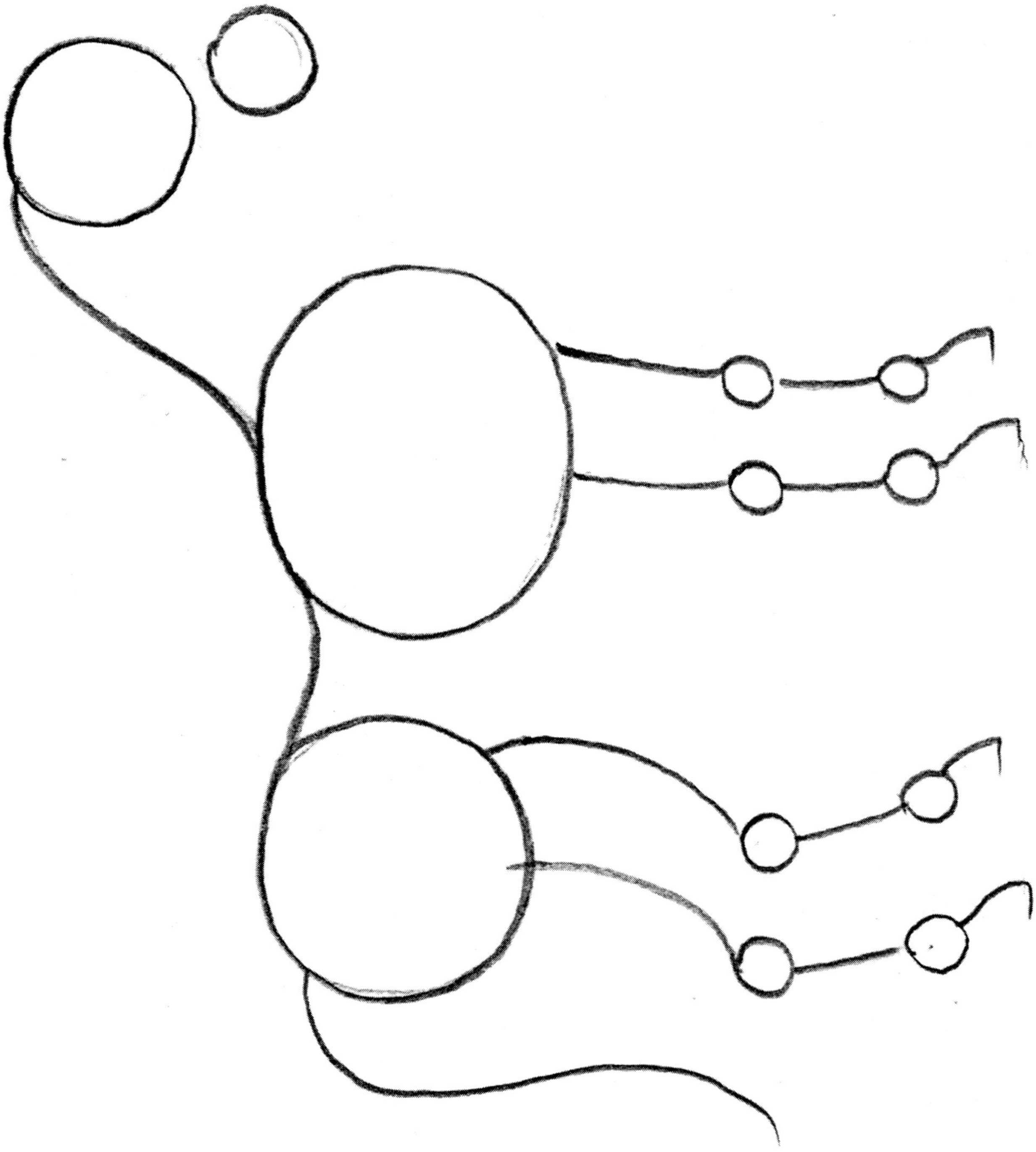

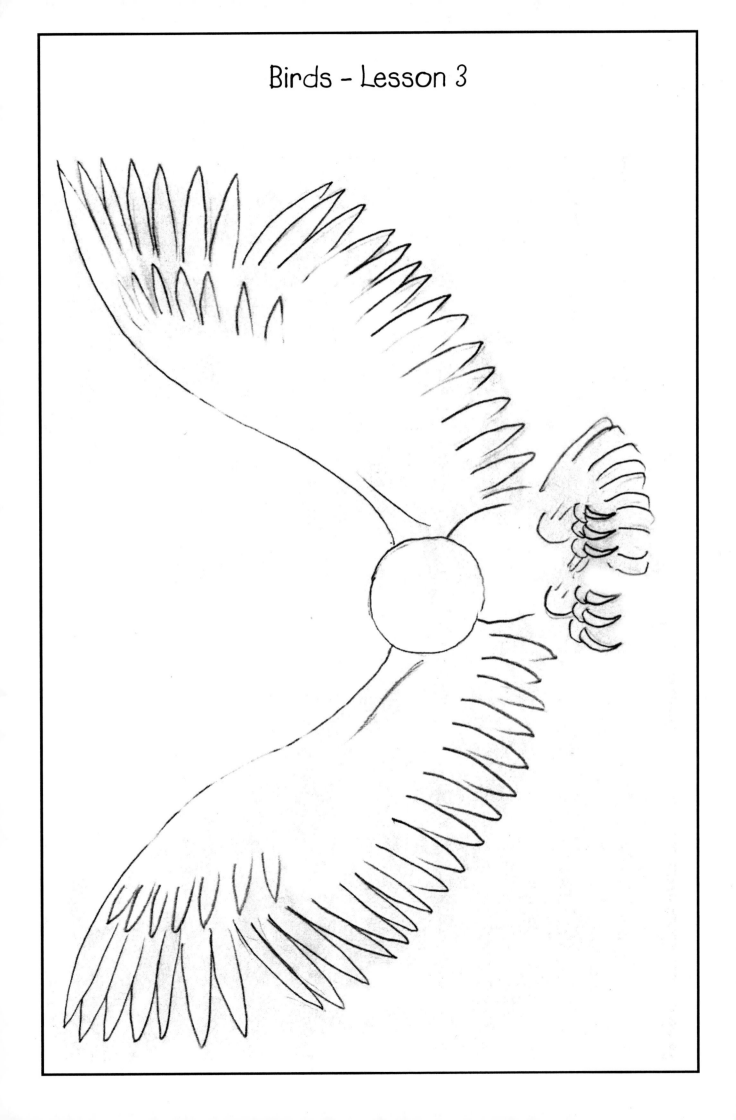

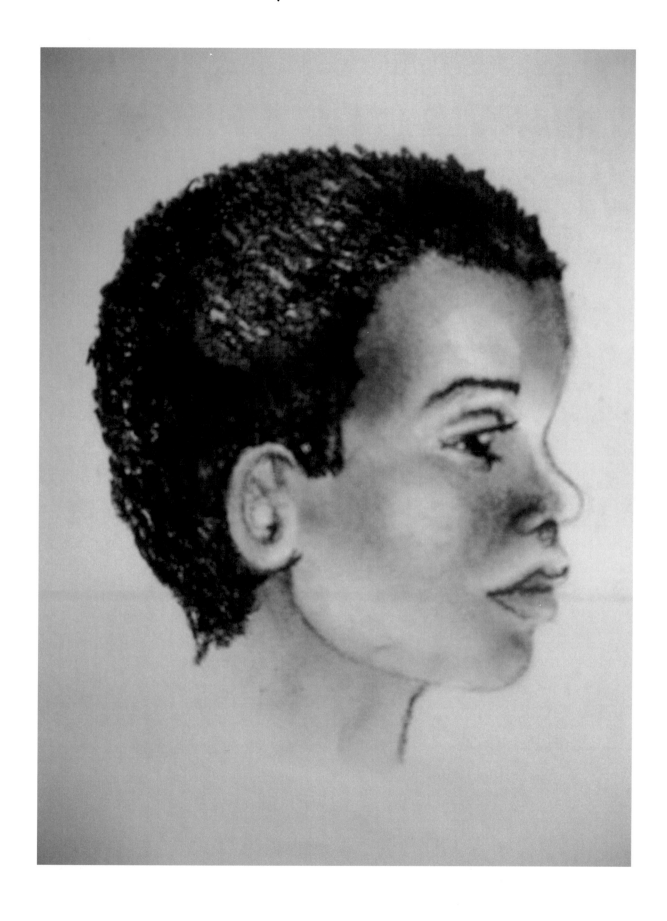

Birds - Lesson 4

Trees - Lesson 3